MUSIC THEORY DICTIONARY

The Language of the Mechanics of Music

MUSIC THEORY DICTIONARY

The Language of the Mechanics of Music

Compiled and Edited
by
DR. W. F. LEE
DEAN AND PROFESSOR OF MUSIC,
SCHOOL OF MUSIC, UNIVERSITY OF MIAMI,
CORAL GABLES, FLORIDA

CHARLES HANSEN EDUCATIONAL
MUSIC AND BOOKS

Library of Congress Catalog Card Number: 65-28888

Made in U.S.A.

PREFACE

THE *Music Theory Dictionary* contains over 3,000 musical terms frequently used by students and teachers of the elements of music, such as Theory, Harmony, Counterpoint, Orchestration, Conducting, Score Reading, Arranging and Composition. This newly revised edition meets the requirements of music theory students and teachers at all levels with simple, easy-to-understand definitions and supplementary materials, including charts, examples and tables. The *Music Theory Dictionary* may be used in collaboration with any standard music theory text or system. It is a *vocabulary of the language of the mechanics of music.*

The terms which are included represent the nomenclature and terminology of past and present-day music theorists and musicians. It is recommended that this book be used as an every-day reference and study guide; not necessarily as a lexicon in the strictly scientific sense of the word. The reader's attention is called to the supplementary material found in Tables I through XXII. In these Tables an attempt has been made to include as much concrete and specific information as space allows. Both the Dictionary and the Tables should prove invaluable to High School, Conservatory, College and University students and teachers.

Grateful acknowledgement is made to my former students in undergraduate and graduate theory classes for providing the inspiration to complete this project. To Messrs. Alfred Reed and Harry Dexter, and my colleagues in the Division of Theory-Composition at this institution I extend sincerest thanks, for making suggestions and proofing the manuscript.

W. F. LEE,
Coral Gables, Florida,
1965.

LIST OF TABLES

— A —

A (*It.*)—By, at, for, etc. In English, A is the sixth note of the scale of C, and the first note of the scale of *a* minor.
A 440 (acoustics)—a^1, equal to 440 vibrations per second, is unanimously adopted as the standard pitch.
Ab (*Ger.*)—Off (in organ music).
A ballata (*It.*)—In ballad style.
Abbandono (*It.*)—With abandon, or passionate expression.
Abgemessen (*Ger.*)—In strict time.
Absolute music—Music composed completely for music's sake without reference to non-musical implications.
Absolute pitch—A highly developed ability to quickly compare an audible impression with acoustic archetypes stored in the memory.
Absorption (acoustics)—The weakening of sound waves through incomplete reflection.
Academic counterpoint—(*See Strict counterpoint.*)
A Cappella (*It.*)—Unaccompanied.
A capriccio (*It.*)—In a capricious style.
Accelerando (*It.*)—Accelerating; increasing the speed.
Accent—The stress of one tone over others. (*See Agogic accent*, *Metric accent*, *etc.*)
Accent of weight—The principal rhythmic accent which corresponds with the end of a musical phrase.
Accessory tone—(*See Non-harmonic tone.*) (*See Table XI.*)
Acciaccatura (*It.*)—A short appoggiatura or grace note sounded simultaneously with the following note. (*See Table XII.*)
Accidentals—Music symbols placed at the left side of the head of a note to raise, lower, or return to normal the pitch of a note. Ex.: sharp (♯); flat (♭); natural (♮); double sharp (𝄪); double flat (♭♭).
Accompanied canon—A canon in which one or more " free " voices (i.e. not part of the canon itself) are employed, to enhance the over-all musical effect.
Accompaniment, motivic—Occurs when a melody is accompanied by motivic material in all of the other voices.
Accompanying voice (free voice)—In a fugue, the voice which accompanies the subject.
Accord (*Fr.*)—A chord, consonance.
Accordion—A musical instrument, the tone of which is produced by the inspiration and respiration of a pair of bellows acting upon metallic reeds.
Acht (*Ger.*)—Eight.
Acoustics—The science dealing with sound and the treatment thereof.
Action—The mechanism of an organ or pianoforte.
Active chord—The dominant chord as opposed to the tonic chord which is a repose chord.
Acute form—The form of the minor scale in which the sixth and seventh scale degrees are raised one semitone. (*See Table XV.*)
Adagietto (*It.*)—A tempo somewhat less slow than adagio, or a short piece in adagio tempo.
Adagio (*It.*)—A slow tempo, slower than andante, but not so slow as largo.
Adagio assai (*It.*)—Very slowly.
Adagio cantabile (*It.*)—Very slow and sustained, as if being sung.

A deux (*Fr.*)—For two instruments or voices.
A deux mains (*Fr.*)—For two hands.
Adjunct—Closely related, by step.
Ad Libitum (Ad Lib) (*Lat.*)—" At will." Gives freedom with regard to rhythm, tempo, inclusion or omission of some voice or instrument, or the extemporizing of a cadenza or section.
A dur (*Ger.*)—A Major.
Aeolian Harp—A stringed instrument so constructed as to give forth musical sounds when exposed to a current of air.
Aeolian Mode (*See Mode*)—The same as our natural minor scale or descending melodic minor. (*See Table X.*)
Aeolian tones (acoustics)—Tones formed by moving air when it passes around, for example, a pole or wire.
Affabile (*It.*)—Pleasing; affably; agreeably.
Affettivo (*It.*)—Affecting, pathetic.
Affettuosamente (*It.*), **Affetuoso** (*It.*)—Affectionately.
Affettuoso (*It.*)—With tender expression.
Afflitto (*It.*)—Sorrowfully, mournfully.
Affrettando (*It.*)—Hurrying, quickening the tempo.
Agevole (*It.*)—Lightly, easily.
Agilita (*It.*)—Agility, lightness.
Agitato (*It.*)—Agitated, restless, hurried.
Agnus Dei (*Lat.*)—One of the parts of a Mass.
Agogic Accent—An accent effected not by dynamic stress or by higher pitch, but by longer duration of the note.
Agréments (*Fr.*)—Embellishments for spinet or harpsichord.
Air—Tune, melody.
Air varié (*Fr.*)—Air with variations.
Air waves (acoustics)—Waves which are produced by any disturbance or by something which is vibrating in only one line of motion.
Ais (*Ger.*)—A-sharp.
Ais dur (*Ger.*)—"A" sharp major.
Akkord (*Ger.*)—A chord.
Al (*It.*)—To. Contracts with the definite article to various forms, such as alla, allo, alle, agli.
Alberti bass—Idiomatic figures of accompaniment for the left hand in keyboard music, consisting of broken chords.
Album leaf—A short and simple piece.
Alcuna (*It.*)—Some, a little.
Al fine (*It.*)—To the end.
Al fine, e poi la coda (*It.*)—To the place marked fine, then to the coda.
Alla (*It.*)—To the, at the, in the style of.
Alla breve (*It.*)—Originally 4/2 meter, each measure being equal to a breve, or double whole note. Now usually 2/2 meter (₵).
Alla Marcia (*It.*)—In march style.
Allargando (*It.*)—Growing broad; slower.
Alle (*Ger.*)—All: Alle Instrumente, all the instruments.
Allegramente (*It.*)—Gaily, joyfully.
Allegretto (*It.*)—Light, cheerful; like allegro, but a little less fast.
Allegrissimo (*It.*)—A little faster than Allegro.
Allegro (*It.*)—Quick, lively; rapid and cheerful.
Alleluia (*Lat.*)—An invitation to praise.
Allemande (*Fr.*)—A German dance in 3/4 meter, like the Landler.

Al loco (*It.*)—A term which is used to counter-order a previous direction, to play an octave higher or lower. A direction to a violinist to return from a shift to his previous position.
Allmählich (*Ger.*)—Gradually, little by little.
All'ottavo (8va . . .) (*It.*)—Indicates those tones that are to be played eight notes or an octave higher or lower than written, depending on where placed.
All' unisono (*It.*)—In unison (or octaves).
Al segno (*It.*)—Return to the sign.
Alt (*It.*)—High; with sopranos, the octave extending from two-line *g* to three-line *f*.
Alteration—The raising or lowering of a note by means of a sharp or flat, thereby altering the chord structure.
Altered chord—A diatonic chord that has been altered by raising or lowering one or more of its elements (root, third, fifth, or seventh) a half step but has not changed the tonality.
Alternating Note—(*See Auxiliary tone.*) (*See Table XI.*)
Altissimo (*It.*)—Highest; the octave above the alt.
Alto (*Fr.*)—Viola.
Alto (*It.*)—High; in former times a high part above the tenor; now applied to the lowest female voices. Another name for the viola.
Alto clef (𝄡)—Usually used by the viola player in modern notation. Third line indicates c^1. (*See Table VII.*)
Alto range (*voice*)—(*See Table XVI.*)
Amabile (*It.*)—Amiable, graceful, gentle.
Ambitus—The range of the melodies of the Gregorian Chant.
Ame (*Fr.*)—Sound post of a violin.
A mezzo voce (*It.*)—In a subdued tone.
Am Frosch (*Ger.*)—At the frog.
Am Griffbrett (*Ger.*)—On the fingerboard.
A moll (*Ger.*)—"A" minor.
Amorosamente (*It.*)—Tenderly, amorously.
Amoroso (*It.*)—Tenderly, lovingly.
Amplitude (acoustics)—The difference between the high and low phases of a sound wave or sound cycle. Usually expressed in pressure as it affects the ear drum. Determines the loudness of sound.
An (*Ger.*)—On; to.
Anacrusis (*Gr.*)—Another term for up-beat which indicates a melody or note beginning with an incomplete measure, beginning one or two beats before the first complete measure.
Analyzing—The process of recognizing the relation of structural details of a unified whole. It is primarily recognition of design.
Ancora (*It.*)—Again, once more, yet.
Andante (*It.*)—A slow, even tempo; literally, "going."
Andantino (*It.*)—A little less slow than andante.
Anfänger (*Ger.*)—A beginner.
Anhang (*Ger.*)—A coda; an appendix.
Animato (*It.*)—Animated; with spirit.
Animé (*Fr.*)—Animated, spirited.
Animoso (*It.*)—In an animated manner; lively, energetic.
Anmuthig (*Ger.*)—Agreeable, sweet.
A-rhythm—Abandonment of the specific rhythmical impulse.
Ansatz (*Ger.*)—Attack. Adjustment of the lips of a wind instrument player,

also adjustment of the mouth to the position required for the production of a vocal phrase.

Anschlag (*Ger.*)—Touch, as applied to piano and other keyed instruments.

Anschwellen (*Ger.*)—To increase in loudness; crescendo.

Answer—The second entry of the Subject in the exposition of a fugue.

Antecedent (*See Period*)—The first phrase of a period or announcing phrase.

Anthem—A composition for voices, with or without instrumental accompaniment, enjoined by the Ritual of the Anglican Church.

Anticipation (*See Non-harmonic*)—A non-harmonic tone which might be considered the opposite of a suspension. It is sounded in the melody before the chord in which it fits is heard. (*See Table XI.*)

Anti-climax note—In counterpoint, there will usually be found in the contour of a melodic line a high and a low note which are not repeated. The low note is the anti-climax note.

Antinode (acoustics)—Pertaining to a vibrating string, the point of widest vibration.

Antiphon (Antiphone)—Responsive or alternate. A short statement from the Scripture.

Antiphonal—In the style of an antiphon. A collection of antiphons.

Antiphony—Singing by double choir of divided choir of alternate verses of a psalm or anthem.

Anwachsend (*Ger.*)—Swelling; crescendo.

Aperto (*It.*)—Open.

Appassionamento (*It.*)—With strong passion or emotion.

Appassionato (*It.*)—Passionate, intense.

Appoggiando (*It.*)—Leaning on or supported. Similar to the appoggiatura or portamento.

Appoggiatura (*It.*)—A melodic ornament. The accented (long) appoggiatura, written as a small note, is accented and borrows time value from the note it precedes. The short appoggiatura (grace note) is usually written as a small eight or sixteenth note with a slanting stroke through the hook and stem. A non-chord tone usually located in a metrically strong position. (*See Table XI.*)

Appoggiatura chord—Several appoggiature sounding together.

Appoggiatura seventh—The non-harmonic tone that occurs when the chord seventh is approached by leap from the chord fifth.

A punta d'arco (*It.*)—With the point of the bow.

A punto (*It.*)—In exact time.

Arabeske, arabesque—A piece with a noticeable design of tonal embroidery.

Arabic numerals—Figures used to identify scale degrees. Ex.: 1, 2, 3, 4, 5, 6, 7. Also used to identify inversions of triads and seventh chords. Ex.: 6, 6, 7, 6, 4, 4, etc.
4 5 3 2

A quatre mains (*Fr.*)—For four hands.

Arcato (*It.*)—Played with the bow.

Archaistic scales—Scales, generally diatonic, which are fixed or stylized patterns of modal alteration.

Archet (*Fr.*)—A violin bow.

Arch form (bow form)—Form which is often utilized in fugues in ABA design.

Arco (*It.*)—Bow, of violins, etc.

Ardente (*It.*)—Ardent, fiery, vehement.

Aria (*It.*)—An air; a song; a tune; sung by a single voice either with or without an accompaniment.

Arioso (*It.*)—A short piece like an aria, but less symmetrical.
Armonioso (*It.*)—Harmonious.
Arpa (*It.*)—Harp.
Arpa doppia (*It.*)—The double action harp.
Arpeggio (*It.*)—Tones of a chord that are sung or played in succession rather than simultaneously.
Arrangement—The adaptation of a composition for instruments other than those for which it was originally written. Music which has been transferred from one medium to another.
Arranger—One who transfers music from one medium to another.
Arsis—The accented beat in a two-beat group.
Articolato (*It.*)—Articulated.
Articulation—In performance, the clear and distinct rendering of the tones; the art of distinct pronunciation.
Artificial invertible counterpoint—Invertible counterpoint which utilizes intervals rather than the octave or its multiples.
As (*Ger.*)—A-flat.
As dur (*Ger.*)—"A" flat.
As moll (*Ger.*)—Key of A flat minor.
Assai (*It.*)—Very, extremely, much.
Assez (*Fr.*)—Fairly.
A-string—The second string of a violin; the first of a viola, or 'cello; the third of a double bass; the fifth of a guitar.
A tempo (*It.*)—In the original speed.
Athematicism—The absence of clearcut themes.
A-thematic music—Music which is not based on thematic or motivic consistency, but music in which the course develops freely without using the affinity of thematic shapes as a structural bond.
Attaca (*It.*)—Attack, start, go on, begin the next.
Attacca subito (*It.*)—Commence at once.
Attack—Promptness and decision in beginning a phrase.
Atonality—Absence of a tonal center.
Attendant chords—Any degree of the scale may be preceded by its own dominant harmony without weakening the fundamental tonality. These temporarily formed dominant chords are sometimes referred to as attendant chords.
Attendant keys—Relative keys. Attendant keys in a scale are the relative minor or major, the dominant and subdominant and their relative minors and majors. (*See Table IX.*)
Attributes of sound (acoustics)—Pitch, intensity, duration, extensity, overtone structure (timbre).
Aubade (*Fr.*)—A morning song, literally a dawn song.
Aufgeregt (*Ger.*)—With agitation.
Aufgeweckt (*Ger.*)—Brisk, lively.
Aufschwung (*Ger.*)—Soaring, elevation.
Augmentation—The lengthening of note values in a melodic line.
Augmentation dot—A dot which adds to a note one-half of its rhythmic value.
Augmented interval—A perfect interval that is made a half-step larger. (*See Table VIII.*)
Augmented-major seventh (AM7)—A chord comprised of an augmented triad and a major seventh interval above the root. (*See Table XIV.*)
Augmented-minor seventh (Am7)—A chord comprised of an augmented triad and a minor seventh interval above the root. (*See Table XIV.*)

Augmented second (interval)—An interval comprised of three semi-tones. (*See Table VIII.*)
Augmented sixth chord—A chord created by use of the minor sixth degree and the chromatically raised fourth degree. (*See Italian sixth*, *French sixth*, *German sixth, etc.*)
Augmented triad—A triad comprised of a major third and an augmented fifth. (*See Table XIV.*)
Aural Analysis—Practice of analyzing music through the ear.
Ausdruck (*Ger.*)—Expression.
Ausgabe (*Ger.*)—Edition.
Authentic cadence—The cadence composed of the progression from dominant to tonic harmonies.
Authentic melody—A melody covering all of the octave-scale above the given tonic.
Authentic mode—In Modal music, indicating that the melodic line lies mainly between the Final (Tonic) and its higher (or lower) octave.
Author's harmony—The usage by a composer of another composer's harmonic progression.
Auxiliary chord—A chord in which two or three auxiliaries occur at the same time. (*See Auxiliary tones.*)
Auxiliary note—A note not essential to the harmony or melody. (*See Table XI.*)
Avec (*Fr.*)—With.
Avec le bois (*Fr.*)—With the wood of the bow.
Auxiliary scales—The scales of relative or attendant keys. (*See Table X.*)
Auxiliary tones—Non-harmonic tones which leave a chord tone stepwise and return immediately to the same chord tone. Often referred to as neighboring tones. (*See Table XI.*)

— B —

B—The seventh note of the scale of C major. In German, B means B-flat.
Bacchetta di spugna (*It.*)—With soft stick.
Bacchette di legno (*It.*)—With hard sticks.
Background of a beat (acoustics)—Fundamental pulsations found within a beat. The natural division of the beat into two or three parts.
Badinage (*Fr.*)—Playfulness.
Bagatelles (*Fr.*)—Sketches, short pieces, trifles.
Bagpipe—A very ancient wind-instrument of Eastern origin.
Baguette d'éponge (*Fr.*)—With soft stick.
Baguettes en bois (*Fr.*)—With hard sticks.
Balance—In four-part writing, the art of harmonically spacing all voices. In performance, proper balancing between vocal or instrumental voices.
Ballad—A song, short and simple, designed to suit a popular audience. Usually in a descriptive form.
Ballade (*Ger.*), **Ballata** (*It.*)—Originally a dance tune. In instrumental music it may be as elaborate as a Chopin " Ballade."
Ballad-opera—An opera made up of simple songs.
Ballet (*Fr.*)—A pantomime story with musical accompaniment. A musical production which utilizes dancers and instrumental music. A composition.
Balletto (*It.*)—A ballet.
Banjo—A five-stringed instrument with long neck, whose sound is reinforced by a parchment covered hoop.
Barcarola (*It.*), **Barcarolle** (*Fr.*)—A song or air sung by the Venetian gondoliers.

Bar, double—Heavy double lines drawn vertically through the staff, dividing off different parts or designating the end of a composition. Dots placed on either side of a double bar mean that preceding or following measures are to be repeated. (*See Table XIII.*)

Bariton (*Fr.*), **Baritone** (*It.*), **Baritone**—A male voice between the bass and tenor. (*See Table XVI.*)

Baritone clef—Third line indicates small *f.* (*See Table VII.*)

Bar-lines—Lines dividing a certain number of beats into measures. The bar-line also indicates the position of the main accent.

Barline displacement—The adding of rhythmic interest by the use of ties over the bar-lines in order to displace the natural strong beats of a measure.

Barre (*Fr.*)—In lute or guitar playing, the stopping of several or all the strings with the left hand forefinger.

Bars—Vertical lines drawn on musical staves to mark off measures. Now used to denote the measures also.

Bass (*Ger.*)—In musical composition, the lowest of the parts.

Bassklarinette (*Ger.*)—Bass Clarinet.

Bass clef—The F clef on the fourth line. (*See Table VII.*)

Bass law—The lowest note of any chord is impelled by an instinctive desire to move a perfect fifth lower or a perfect fourth higher.

Basset Horn—A transposing instrument of the clarinet order.

Basson (*Fr.*)—Bassoon.

Basso (*It.*)—The lowest part; a bass singer. (*See Table XVI.*)

Bass obbligato (*It.*)—A bass part indispensible to the accompaniment.

Basso buffo (*It.*)—A comic bass singer.

Basso Continuo (*It.*)—A guide to the harmonic background of the keyboard music in order to fill in missing parts or to reinforce weak ones. The continual or figured bass in 18th century music. (*See figured bass.*)

Basso Giusto (*It.*)—A basso cantante, lyrical bass, as opposed to basso profundo, deep and powerful bass.

Basso Ostinato (*It.*)—A short bass figure, one or two measures in length, which is repeated continuously throughout a passage or composition.

Bassoon—A wood-wind instrument of the oboe or double reed family.

Basso profundo (*It.*)—A very deep bass voice.

Bass range (voice)—(*See Table XVI.*)

Bass tuba—A brass instrument of low pitch. Compass of four octaves.

Bass voice—The lowest male voice. (*See Table XVI.*)

Baton (*Fr.*)—A conductor's stick or wand.

Battuta (*It.*)—A beat; a measure. A battuta, in strict time.

B dur (*Ger.*)—B flat major.

Beam—Used in place of flags to show the groups of notes which are to be sung on one syllable. In instrumental music, beams are used to group notes into metric patterns.

Beat—The temporal unit of a composition, as is indicated by the up-and-down movements of the conductor's hand. An acoustical phenomenon resulting from the interference of two sound waves of slightly different frequency.

Beat tone (acoustics)—Beat tones are produced when beats from strong sources follow each other at the rate of about twenty or more per second, and particularly when they are produced by two loud tones on the same instrument, instead of by two different instruments.

Bebung (*Ger.*)—A shaking; a vibration; also a German organ stop.

Bécarre (*Fr.*)—Sign called a natural.

Becken (*Ger.*)—Cymbals.

Bel canto (*It.*)—Literally " well sung." A pure and sympathetic legato, the opposite of bravura, coloratur, agilita, etc.
Bell—The lower termination of any tubular musical instrument which assumes the form of a bell.
Bellicoso (*It.*)—In a martial, war-like style.
Bémol (*Fr.*)—Any flat.
Bémolle (*It.*)—Any flat.
Ben, bene (*It.*)—Well, thoroughly.
Benedictus (*Lat.*)—One of the parts in a Mass.
Ben marcato (*It.*)—Well and clearly marked.
Berceuse (*Fr.*)—Lullaby.
Bes (*Ger.*)—Note B double flat.
Bestimmt (*Ger.*)—With energy; con energia.
Bewegt (*Ger.*)—Rather fast; with motion.
Binary form—Music which is divided into two parts.
Binaural sense (acoustics)—A faculty that our ears perform with fair ease in telling us from what direction a sound comes.
Bind—A tie. Designated by a curved line. The same sign, when over two or more notes on different degrees, is called a slur. (*See Table XIII.*)
Bipartite fugue—A fugue constructed according to a two-part plan.
Bis (*Lat.*)—Twice; to be repeated; continued.
B moll (*Ger.*)— B flat minor.
Bogen (*Ger.*)—Bow, of violins, etc. Also a slur or tie.
Bolero (*Sp.*)—Spanish dance in 3/4 meter; also called Cachuca.
Bombardon—A large, deep-toned brass instrument.
Bones—Pieces of wood or bone, held two in each hand and struck together for the purpose of marking time. Used especially for negro minstrel music.
Bordone (*It.*), **Bourdon** (*Fr.*)—An organ stop, consisting of stopped wooden pipes, generally of sixteen-foot tone.
Borrowed chords—Chords not found within the diatonic scale structure. Secondary dominants, etc.
Borrowed tones—Altered tones in chords which retain their diatonic functions. They are ordinarily due to a temporary interchange of mode.
Bouché (*Fr.*)—Closed, applied either in vocal music to ask for humming with closed mouth, or in instrumental music as, for example, stopped Horn.
Bourdon (*Fr.*)—A set of large organ pipes. A drone bass accompaniment.
Bourrée (*Fr.*)—An old French dance.
Bow—A contrivance of wood and horsehair, employed to set the strings of the violin, etc. in vibration.
Bow form—(*See Arch form.*)
Bowing—The art of using the bow; playing with the bow. " The Bowing " also refers to the marks used to guide the player.
Brace—A figure used to connect two or more ståves which are to be performed together. (*See Table XIII.*)
Bracket—Used instead of a beam in some cases, with a number added to indicate how many notes are to be sung in a particular figure.
Brass band—So called when all reed instruments are omitted.
Bratsche (*Ger.*)—Viola.
Bravura (*It.*)—Spirit, skill, requiring dexterity.
Break—The change between the head and chest register in voices. The change between lower and upper registers on some instruments, such as the Clarinet.
Breath sign—(*See Table XIII.*)
Breit (*Ger.*)—Broad, stately.

Breve—Originally meaning a short note; equal to two whole notes. (*See Table III.*)
Brevis—A note which fills a whole measure in 4/2 or 2/1 meter (𝅜).
Bridge—A piece of wood which, on instruments having a sound-board or resonance box, performs the double duty of raising the strings and at terminating at one end their vibrating portion.
Brillante (*It.*)—Brilliant, sparkling.
Brindisi (*It.*)—Drinking song in 3/4 or 3/8 meter, often written to resemble the Jodl.
Brio (*It.*)—Sprightliness, spirit.
Brisé (*Fr.*)—Broken chords, arpeggios.
Broken chords, broken octaves—Chords or octaves whose notes are played in succession and not simultaneously.
Buffo (*It.*)—Comic; a singer who takes comic parts.
Bugle—A brass horn of straight or curved form. Generally used for infantry calls.
Burlando (*It.*)—Joking, jesting.
Burlesque—An extravaganza tending to excite laughter by farcial representations.

— C —

C—The first note in the scale of *c*. The sign for common time (4/4) is not really a *C* (Tempus imperfectum), but two-thirds of a circle.
Cabaletta (*It.*)—A melody in rondo form, the theme often repeated with elaborate variations.
Cachuca (*Sp.*)—A Spanish dance, similar to the Bolero.
Cadence—A close in melody or harmony ending a period, section or entire piece. The chord progression at the close of a phrase. (*See Authentic cadence, Perfect authentic cadence, Imperfect authentic cadence, Half cadence, Deceptive cadence, Plagal cadence, Perfect plagal cadence, Imperfect plagal cadence, Phrygian cadence.*)
Cadential modulation—The assumption of a new key by simply beginning on its tonic after a perfect authentic cadence in the old key.
Cadential six-four chord—A dominant chord in which the sixth and fourth form appoggiature to the fifth and third respectively. It has the rhythmic nature of strong-to-weak.
Cadenza (*It.*)—An ornamental solo passage introduced near the end of a composition either written by the composer or extemporized by the performer. An extended section in free improvisatory style giving the player or singer a chance to exhibit his technical brilliance.
Caisse roulante (*Fr.*)—Tenor drum.
Calando (*It.*)—Becoming softer and slower.
Calcando (*It.*)—Hurrying the time.
Calmato (*It.*)—Tranquil, quiet.
Caloroso (*It.*)—Warm, animated.
Cambiata—An interpolated tone between a dissonant tone, or tendency tone, and its resolution. (*See Table XI.*)
Campane (*It.*)—Bells or chimes.
Campane in aria (*It.*)—Bells in the air.
Campanelli (*It.*)—Glockenspiel.
Cancel—Natural (♮). Organ stop.
Cancion (*Sp.*)—Song.

Canon—Musical Imitation in the strictest form. A strict and extended application of the stretto principle. It may occur at any pitch or rhythmic interval.
Canon crancrizan (Crab canon)—Canon in which voices are sounded forward and backward simultaneously. Also referred to as a Retrograde canon.
Canonic imitation—Strict imitation.
Canon in augmentation—Occurs when the second voice of the canon is written in note values longer than those of the first voice.
Canon in diminution—Occurs when the second voice of the canon is written in notes shorter than the values in the first voice.
Cantabile (*It.*)—In a singing style, smoothly.
Cantare (*It.*)—To sing; to celebrate.
Cantata (*It.*)—Vocal work with instrumental accompaniment—shorter than an Oratorio.
Canticle—One of the non-metrical hymns of praise and jubilation in the Bible. A song or hymn in honor of God.
Cantilena (*It.*)—The melody of a song or piece; a melodious song, piece or passage.
Canto (*It.*)—A song, a chant, a melody. The upper voice-part is concerted music, so called because it has the melody.
Cantus firmus (*Lat.*)—Fixed melody; frequently used as a thematic basis for polyphonic works through the 18th century.
Canzone (*It.*)—A song, folk-song; also a part-song in madrigal style.
Capo (*It.*)—The beginning, the top or head.
Capotasto (*It.*)—A mechanical contrivance by which the pitch of the whole of the strings of such instruments like the guitar, etc., are raised simultaneously. In English generally called Capo d'astro.
Cappella (*It.*)—A chapel or church. A musical band.
Capriccio (*It.*)—Instrumental music in free form.
Capriccioso (*It.*)—Capriciously, fancifully.
Caprice (*Fr.*), **Capriccio** (*It.*), **Capriccioso** (*It.*)—Whimsical, humorous, fanciful. A composition somewhat irregular in form.
Caressant (*Fr.*)—Caressing, tenderly.
Carezzando (*It.*), **Carezzovole** (*It.*)—In a caressing and tender manner.
Carillon—A set of bells so arranged as to be played by hand or by mechanical finger keys.
Carita (*It.*)—Feeling, tenderness.
Carol—(1) a song; (2) a song of praise, applied to a type of songs sung at Christmas time.
Castagnette (*It.*)—Castanets.
Castagnettes (*Fr.*)—Castanets.
Castanet—A pair of small pieces of hard wood, which are stuck together in order to yield a percussive effect.
Castrato (*It.*)—An adult male singer with female voice range.
Catch—A canon or round for three or more voices.
Catgut—The name given to the material of which many musical instrument strings are made.
Cavatina (*It.*)—A melody of a simple form. A song without a second part and a " Da capo."
C clef—(*See Table VII.*)
C dur (*Ger.*)—The key of C major.
Celesta (*It.*) (*Ger.*)—Celesta. (*Fr.*)—Céleste.
Celesta—An instrument consisting of steel tuning forks and struck with mallets through the medium of a keyboard.

Céleste (*Fr.*)—Celestial, heavenly; " voix céleste," an organ stop.
'Cello (*It.*)—An abbreviation of violoncello.
Cembalo (*It.*)—A harpsichord.
Central tone—Referring to the key tone or tonic.
Cents (acoustics)—A unit of scientific and exact method of measuring intervals in music. A cent is one-hundredth of a semitone in the well-tempered scale.
Ces (*Ger.*)—C-flat.
Ces dur (*Ger.*)—The key of C flat major.
Cesura—The section between a strong (masculine) and weak (feminine) period.
Chaconne (*Fr.*)—A Spanish dance. Also, an instrumental piece consisting of a series of variations above a ground bass.
Chain suspensions—Term used to describe the occurence of several suspensions occuring consecutively.
Chamber Music—Most frequently applied to concerted compositions of instrumental music in the form of string quartets or quintets. Vocal or instrumental pieces suitable for performance in a chamber-room, as opposed to a concert hall.
Chance music—Music which permits the performer to play various sections of a composition in any order he chooses.
Changing-chord—A chord occuring on thc strong beat which contains notes dissonant to the bass.
Change of Mode—Occurs when the major tonality changes to minor tonality, or vice versa, on the same tonal center. Ex.: From C major to c minor.
Change of quality—Refers to certain changes not readily explained either by change of mode or dominant embellishment.
Changing tones—Non-harmonic tones dependent upon the first tone of an interval and left by skip.
Chanson (*Fr.*)—Song.
Chansonette (*Fr.*)—A little song.
Chant (*Fr.*)—General denomination for liturgical music in the character of plainsong, monophonic, unaccompanied, and in free rhythm.
Characteristic tone—Leading tone.
Chasse (*Fr.*)—Hunting.
Che (*It.*)—Then; that.
Chest register—Register used predominantly by all male singers.
Chiarezza (*It.*)—Clearness, purity, neatness.
Chica—A dance popular among Spaniards.
Chiuso (*It.*)—Stopped horn.
Chladni's figures (acoustics)—Figures which are revealed by sprinkling a little fine sand or sawdust over a membrane. When set into vibration, the sand is violently agitated where the vibration-loops are located, and collects at all nodal points or lines.
Choeur (*Fr.*)—Chorus, choir.
Choir—Company of singers; part of a church appropriated to singers.
Choir Organ—One of the divisions of the organ, the manual for which is generally the lowest.
Chor (*Ger.*)—Chorus, choir; a number of instruments of the same kind.
Chorale—A hymn tune or sacred tune.
Chorale fantasia—A chorale in extremely free form.
Chorale figuration—A species of contrapuntal variation woven around a chorale melody which may or may not be embellished.
Chorale fughetta—A small fugue in which the subject is derived from a chorale melody.

Chorale fugue—A fugue in which the subject is derived from a chorale melody.
Chorale melody—(*See Cantus Firmus.*)
Chorale motet—A chorale in which each motive is announced in fugal fashion.
Chorale prelude—Generally a chorale for four voices which contains the chorale melody (Cantus Firmus), motivic material derived from the chorale melody and additional accompanying material.
Chord—Simultaneous sound of three or more tones. (*See Table XIV.*)
Chord, common—A chord consisting of a fundamental note together with its third and fifth.
Chord connection—The joining together of chords in a harmonic progression.
Chord, dominant—A chord that is found on the dominant of the key in which the music is written.
Chord, inverted—A chord, the notes of which are so dispersed that the root does not appear as the lowest note.
Chord-line melody—A melody which is made up wholly or in large part from tones of the harmony.
Chord of nature—A chord constructed from the natural harmonic series. (*See Table II.*)
Chorus—(1) a body of singers; (2) the refrain of a song; (3) a composition for a body of singers.
Chromatic—(*See Accidental.*)
Chromatic alteration—The raising or lowering of a note by means of one of the following symbols: sharp (♯); flat (♭); natural (♮); double sharp (𝄪); double flat (♭♭).
Chromaticism—The use of melodic or harmonic elements not found in the diatonic sequence.
Chromatic half-step—Two tones one-half step apart with the same letter name. Ex.: B-B flat; G-G sharp; A-A flat.
Chromatic half-tone—Occurs when the two tones involved belong to a single basic tone.
Chromatic mode—The merging into one mode of the chromatic resources of the 19th century.
Chromatic modulation—Modulation involving chromatic progression in one or more parts.
Chromatic passing tones—The effect given in rapid harmonic movement, in which successive diminished sevenths progress by half steps.
Chromatic scale (*See Scale*)—A scale consisting of twelve half-tones to the octave. (*See Table X.*)
Chromatic spelling—The spelling of each chromatic chord in relation to its chord of resolution by using the same letters for the same pitches and different letters for different pitches.
Church modes—Scales employed in medieval church music. (*See Table X.*)
Church modes—Plain song. The kind of music used from time immemorial in worship.
Circle of chords—Each chord functions as the dominant of the following chord a fifth below.
Circle of fifths—A succession of perfect fifths which, in our well-tempered system, return to the initial tone after twelve progressions.
Circle of major keys—Major keys placed on a circle in order of ascending or descending fifths.
Circle of minor keys—Minor keys placed on a circle in order of ascending or descending fifths.

Circle of modes—A circle of modes may be played by starting with the Locrian mode on a tone, and adding one by one the accidentals in the order of sharps.
Circular canon—A canon which terminates in the key 1/2 step higher than that in which it begins.
Cis (*Ger.*)—C-sharp.
Cis-cis (*Ger.*)—Note C double sharp.
Cis dur (*Ger.*)—Key C sharp major.
Cis moll (*Ger.*)—Key C sharp minor.
Clarabella—An eight-foot soft organ stop.
Clarinet or Clarionet (a little clarion)—A wind instrument with a beating reed.
Clarinette (*Fr.*)—Clarinet.
Clarinette Basse (*Fr.*)—Bass Clarinet.
Clarinetto (*It.*)—Clarinet.
Clarinetto Basso (*It.*)—Bass Clarinet.
Clarino (*It.*), **Clarion**—A trumpet, also an organ stop of four-foot pitch.
Clavichord—One of the predecessors of the piano, the mechanism employing metal wedges rather than hammers.
Clavecin (*Fr.*)—The harpsichord, or the spinet.
Clavier (*Fr.*), **Clavier** (*Ger.*)—The keyboard of pianoforte, organ, etc. Germans call the piano " Clavier " or " Klavier."
Clavier-auszug (*Ger.*)—A pianoforte score.
Clef—From the Latin *Clavin* meaning key. A sign placed at the beginning of the staff to indicate a specific pitch. (*See Table VII.*)
Climax, fugue subject—A point in a fugue which is reached by pitch, rhythmic and harmonic implications.
Climax note—A note of high pitch in a phrase.
Clivis—A kind of neume. (*See Table III.*)
Cloches (*Fr.*)—Bells or chimes.
Close harmony—Occurs when the upper three voices are as close together as possible. Soprano and Tenor are usually never more than an octave apart.
Close structure—Occurs when there is an octave or less between the soprano and tenor.
Closed vocal score—One in which the grand staff is used, with bass and tenor parts on the bass staff and soprano and alto parts on the treble staff.
Closely related key—One in which the tonic triad of the new key is found as a diatonic triad in the original key.
Clusters—When a passage is dominated by chords by seconds and arranged in predominantly uninverted forms so that most of the voices are a second apart, the chords are called clusters.
C moll (*Ger.*)—C minor.
Cochlea (acoustics)—Inner ear.
Coda (*It.*)—Tailpiece or the ending of a passage.
Codetta (*It.*)—A short coda or extra concluding passage usually located in the interior of a composition or movement.
Cogli, Col, Coll', Colla, Colle, Collo (*It.*)—With the.
Colla voce—With the voice.
Col legno (*It.*) (*Ger.*)—With the wood of the bow.
Coloratura (*It.*)—Roulades, embellishments, or ornamental passages in vocal music.
Come (*It.*)—As, like, the same as,
Comma (acoustics)—The difference between a major and minor tone in the natural scale (ratio of 81 to 80).
Commodo (*It.*)—Quietly, without haste.

Common chord—An older term for the major triad. The term used for the pivot chord in modulation, the chord being common both to the original key and to the new key.
Common time—Time with two beats in a bar or any multiple of two beats in a bar. Common time is of two kinds: simple and compound.
Common tone—A tone found in two consecutive chords that occurs in the same relative position in each chord.
Comodo (*It.*)—Quietly, easily, conveniently.
Compass—The range of pitches available to a voice or instrument.
Compass of voices—(*See Tables XVI, XVII and XVIII.*)
Complete cadence—The cadence progression from tonic to subdominant, to dominant, to tonic. (*See Cadence.*)
Complete chord—A chord in which no tone is omitted.
Compound beat—A beat which has a background of three equal pulsations.
Compound harmony—Chords made up of thirds and fourths.
Compound intervals—Intervals larger than an octave.
Compound meters—Meters which use triple units.
Complex pitch (acoustics)—Occurs when two musical tones are sounded together.
Composite wave (acoustics)—Presence of other frequencies varying in their respective intensities in the shape of the wave.
Compressed score—A score in which more than one part is placed on a staff.
Computer music—The use of an automatic high-speed digital computer in actual composition of music. In contrast with electronic music and musique concrete, where new sound media are created, the computer composes pieces that can be played on conventional instruments.
Con (*It.*)—With.
Con Amore (*It.*)—With love.
Concertante (*It.*)—Concert piece.
Concerted music—Music written in parts for several instruments or voices, like trios, quartets, etc.
Concert fugue—A fugue in which there is particular emphasis on brilliance and dramatic effect.
Concertina—The improved accordion invented by Wheatstone in 1829.
Concert Master—The first violinist of an orchestra.
Concerto (*It.*)—A piece of several movements for one or more solo instruments with orchestra—sometimes one solo instrument with piano.
Concerto grosso (*It.*)—A concertino for instruments utilizing a small group of soloists accompanied by full orchestra.
Concertstück (*Ger.*)—A concert-piece; a concerto.
Conduct—To direct a performance of music in a unified musical effort by means of manual and bodily motions.
Conducting frames—(*See Table V.*)
Conjunct degree—The nearest tone in the diatonic or chromatic scale to the given tone.
Conjunct motion—Progression by conjunct intervals. A term used to describe the movement of a single line moving by step.
Consecutive fifths—The parallel movement of any two voices in fifths.
Consecutive imperfect fifths—The moving of two voices from a perfect fifth to a diminished fifth, or vice versa.
Consecutive octaves—The parallel movement of any two voices in octaves.
Consecutive unisons—The parallel movement of any two voices in unison.

Consequent (*See Period*)—The second phrase of a period, the answering phrase, after ending in a full close.
Consonance—A relation or state of relative rest or relaxation between various tones that produces an agreeable effect.
Consonant chord—A chord containing no dissonant interval.
Consonant intervals—All the perfect intervals (unisons, octaves, fourths, fifths), major and minor thirds and sixths.
Consonant triad—A triad based on the relationship of the perfect fifth.
Con sordino (*It.*)—Muted.
Continued bass—Same as figured bass.
Continuo (*It.*)—Constant, continual.
Contra (*Lat.*)—Literally " against." When prefixed to names of instruments means an octave below (Contrabass, Contrabassoon, etc.).
Contralto (*It.*)—Literally, a deeper alto. Often used to mean alto.
Contrapuntal—In the style of counterpoint.
Contrapuntal inversion—A modification of the mirror inversion. The same scale is kept so that while each interval and its inversion have the same general name, the specific names may be different due to the place in the scale occupied by each.
Contrary motion—Occurs when two voices move in opposite directions.
Contrabasso (*It.*)—Double bass.
Contrafagotto (*It.*)—Contra bassoon.
Contra octave—(*See Table I.*)
Contrappunto (*It.*), **Contrapunkt** (*Ger.*)—Counterpoint.
Contrapuntal associate—Used synonomously with counter-subject. (*See Counter-subject.*)
Contrapuntal dissonance—Dissonance created by melodic non-harmonic tones.
Contre (*Fr.*)—Against; contra, counter.
Contre Basse (*Fr.*)—Double bass.
Contre-basson (*Fr.*)—Contra bassoon.
Converting tone—The tone which is used as the initial tone of the descending complementary scale.
Cor (*Fr.*)—Horn.
Cor Anglais (*Fr.*)—English horn.
Coranto (*It.*)—(1) Courante; (2) country dance.
Corda (*It.*)—String. In piano music, una corda (one string) means soft pedal, while tre corde (three strings) means a cessation of the soft pedal.
Corde (*Fr.*)—String.
Cornet, Cornetto (*It.*)—Modern brass instrument, having valves or pistons by means of which a complete chromatic scale can be produced.
Corno (*It.*)—Horn.
Corno Inglese (*It.*)—English horn.
Coro (*It.*)—Chorus.
Corona (*Lat.*)—Pause, i.e., the sign 𝄐, also called Fermata.
Cotillon (*Fr.*)—A lively, French dance.
Counterchords—Derived from a two-part linear frame of single-tone lines.
Counter-exposition—The exposition which follows the regular exposition in a fugue.
Counterpoint—The art of writing independent melodies against each other.
Counter-subject—A melodic idea that appears with the subject in the exposition and later in the fugue.
Coupler—Mechanism which connects pedals with the manuals, or, different manuals of an organ together.

Couplet—In compound meter, two equal notes played in the time of three notes in the regular rhythm.
Courante (*Fr.*)—A Courant, or old French dance in 3/2 meter.
Crab canon—(*See Canon Crancrizan.*)
Cracovienne (*Fr.*)—A Polish dance in 2/4 meter.
Credo (*Lat.*)—One of the movements in a Mass.
Cremona—A violin made at Cremona, Italy.
Crescendo (*It.*)—A gradual increase in power.
Crooks—Short tubes, straight or curved, to be added to horns, cornets, etc. for the purpose of changing the key.
Cross relation—Chromaticism occuring between two different voices in adjacent chords.
Crotchets—Quarter notes. (*See Table III.*)
Csardas (*Hun.*)—Hungarian dance.
Cue—A catch word or phrase. The last notes or words of other parts inserted as a guide to singers or actors who have to make an entry after rests.
Cuivré (*Fr.*)—Brassy.
Cycle (acoustics)—A complete sound wave moving to point of highest displacement through point of lowest displacement and back to point of highest displacement.
Cycle or Cyclical forms—Sonatas, Symphonies and Suites are examples of Cycle forms, because made up of several complete movements and forms. (*See Table XV.*)
Cyclic relationships—Refers to the relationship of chord through the cycle of fifths, cycle of fourths, cycle of thirds, cycle of seconds, etc.
Cymbales (*Fr.*)—Cymbals.
Cymbals—Circular brass plates, which are set in vibration by being struck or by being clashed together.

— D —

D—The second note in the scale of C major. Abbreviation for Da, Dal, or Destra.
Da (*It.*)—From, by, through, etc. Dal, Dalle, etc. are the same.
Da Capo (D.C.) (*It.*)—From the beginning.
Da capo al fine (*It.*)—From the beginning to the sign " fine."
Da Capo al segno (*It.*)—From the beginning to the sign.
Dactylic—A metrical foot with one long and two short syllables.
Dagli, dai, dal, dall', dalla, dalle, dallo (*It.*)—To the, by the, for the, from the, etc.
Dal segno (*It.*)—From the sign 𝄋.
Dal segno al fine (*It.*)—Repeat from the sign to the end; that is, to the place where *fine* is written.
D. C.—(*See Da Capo.*)
D. C. al fine (*It.*)—Literally, from the head. Repetition from beginning to a certain place marked *fine.*
Damper—Moveable pieces of mechanism in a pianoforte, for checking the vibration of the string; (2) damper pedal, the name applied to the " right " pedal on a piano; (3) the mute of a horn or other brass instrument.
Damper weg (*Ger.*)—Take off mute.
D dur (*Ger.*)—D major.
Dead spots (acoustics)—The dead spots in an auditorium may be due to an interference field set up by a source and its reflected echoes. If the sound

waves reaching the ear of a hearer directly from the stage are exactly one-half wave-length " out of phase " with those reaching him through reflection from a near-by wall, that particular pitch is greatly weakened, since the amplitude of the reflected wave is always somewhat less than the direct one.

Decad—Ten-note chord.

Deceptive cadence—A cadence in which the dominant chord does not resolve to the tonic in octave position.

Decibel (acoustics)—Scientific unit for measuring loudness or intensity of sound.

Deciso (*It.*)—Boldly, decidedly.

Declamando (*It.*)—In a declamatory style.

Decoration—Same as ornamentation, coloratura, florid style.

Decrescendo (*It.*)—Gradually diminishing the power.

Decuplet—A group of ten equal notes played in the time usually alloted to eight notes of similar value, or to four notes of the next highest value, in the regular rhythm.

Degrees—The tones of a scale. The degrees are numbered from one to seven.

1. Do, Tonic.
2. Re, Supertonic.
3. Mi, Mediant.
4. Fa, Subdominant.
5. So, Dominant.
6. La, Submediant.
7. Ti, Leading-tone.

Ex: C: 1 2 3 4 5 6 7 8

Delicato (*It.*)—Delicate, smooth.

Demiquaver—A sixteenth note. (*See Table III.*)

Dependent chord—A dissonant chord requiring resolution to a consonant chord.

Dependent tones—The second, fourth, sixth and seventh degrees of the scale.

Derivation—The act of deriving chords from other chords or combination of notes or intervals.

Des (*Ger.*)—D-flat.

Descant—An independent melody which is composed to accompany another melody.

Des dur (*Ger.*)— D flat major.

Des moll (*Ger.*)—D flat minor.

Destra (*It.*)—Right, right hand.

Detaché (*Fr.*)—Detached, staccato, in violin music. A type of bowing in which notes of equal value are bowed singly with slight articulation.

Determinato (*It.*)—Determined, resolute.

Detto (*It.*)—The same.

Development—The evolution or elaboration of a theme, melodically, harmonically or rhythmically.

Di (*It.*)—Of, with from, etc.

Diabolus in musica (*It.*)—Another name for the tritone which was considered, in the 15th and 16th centuries, the " most dangerous " interval.

Diapason—The entire scale or range. A set of organ pipes running through the entire keyboard.

Diapason A—The fifth A counting from the bottom of the piano keyboard. (A-440.)

Diastematic (acoustics)—Method of expressing sound in writing used by musicians. Notation by interval.

Diatonic—An order of tones expressed by the white keys of the piano; concerning scales with progressing degrees of different names.

Diatonic chord—A chord whose tones conform to a diatonic scale.
Diatonic half-step—Two tones one-half step apart with consecutive letter names. Ex: C-D flat, A-G♯, G♯-F .
Diatonic melody—A melody using the materials of the diatonic scale exclusively.
Diatonic modulation—Occurs when the tonality change is effected by means of a pivot chord which is diatonic in both keys.
Diatonic scale—A scale consisting of whole and half-tone steps. (*See Table X.*)
Diatonicized chromaticism—A technique of composition involving twelve tones in an ordered relationship and allowing the composer to use any tone without modulating.
Dictation—The recognition and identification of specific elements of music aurally without reference to the score. It is analysis by ear rather than by eye.
Didymic comma—The smallest interval recognized in music, found by subtracting a major whole tone from a minor whole tone.
Die Hälfte (*Ger.*)—Half a string group.
Dièse, Dièze (*Fr.*)—Any sharp.
Difference tone (acoustics)—See beat tone.
Diffraction (acoustics)—A change in the direction of sound waves caused by the introduction of obstacles around which the waves bend.
Diffusion (acoustics)—The spreading out of sound in spherical waves as it leaves the source.
Diluendo (*It.*)—Dying away into silence.
Diminished—Made less. Smaller than minor or perfect. (*See Table VIII.*)
Diminished-diminished seventh or diminished seventh (d7)—A chord comprised of a diminished triad and a diminished seventh interval above the root. (*See Table XIV.*)
Diminished fifth chord—A chord comprised of a minor third and diminished fifth. (*See Table XIV.*)
Diminished interval—A perfect or minor interval that is made a half-step smaller. (*See Table VIII.*)
Diminished-minor seventh (dm7)—A chord comprised of a diminished triad and a minor seventh interval above the root. (*See Table XIV.*)
Diminished octave—An interval comprising eleven half tones. (*See Table VIII.*)
Diminished seventh chord—A chord comprised of a diminished triad and a diminished seventh interval above the root. (*See Table XIV.*)
Diminished triad—A chord comprised of a minor third and a diminished fifth. (*See Table XIV.*)
Diminuendo (*It.*)—Gradually diminished in power.
Diminution—Refers to the shortening of note values in a melodic line.
Direct motion (*See Motion*)—Occurs when two voices move in the same direction, up or down.
Dis (*Ger.*)—D-sharp.
Discant—Early polyphony with contrary motion in the parts.
Dischord—The result of the formation of dissonant combinations of tones.
Disjunct motion—A term used to describe the movement of a single line moving by skips.
Dismemberment—Refers to the omission or shuffling of chords when a passage is thematically significant and easily retained aurally.
Dis moll (*Ger.*)—D sharp minor.
Dissonance—A relation or state of tension between various tones; generally a disagreeable sound.
Dissonance, harmonic—The adding of a dissonant element to an otherwise constant chord.

Dissonant chord—A chord containing one or more dissonant intervals
Dissonant interval—All seconds, sevenths, ninths, diminished and augmented intervals.
Dissonantal tension—The relative quantity of dissonance, i.e., a major seventh is more dissonant than a major second.
Div. a 3 (*It.*) (*Fr.*)—Divided in three parts.
Divertimento (*It.*), **Divertissement** (*Fr.*)—(1) A light composition for the piano; (2) a suite for instruments.
Divisé (*Fr.*)—Divided.
Divisi (*It.*)—Divided, separated; used when a single group of voices or instruments is to take two or more notes instead of one.
Do (*It.*)—The syllable applied to the tonal center of a scale in singing, etc. In the " fixed " Do system, Do is always C. The French use UT instead of Do in instrumental music.
Doad—Two-note chord.
Dodecaphonic music—A method of composition involving twelve tones which are related only with one another. Used synonomously with the terms *twelve-tone music* and *serial music.*
Dodecuple scale—An independent scale with twelve equally important steps.
Dodecuplet—A group of twelve equal notes, to be played in the time of eight notes of the same kind in the regular rhythm.
Dolce (*It.*)—Sweetly.
Dolente (*It.*)—Mournful, grieving.
Doloroso (*It.*)—Sadly, sorrowfully.
Dominant (*Sol.*)—Referring to the fifth degree of a scale.
Dominant cadence (*See Cadence*)—The cadence progression from dominant to tonic.
Dominant chord—A chord founded on the dominant or fifth note of the scale.
Dominant harmony—The strongest tonal factor in music. Standing alone, it determines the key much more decisively than the tonic chord itself.
Dominant seventh chord—A major-minor seventh chord built on the fifth scale degree in either major and harmonic minor tonality.
Dominant triad—The triad which occurs on the dominant degree.
D moll (*Ger.*)—Key of D minor.
Dopo (*It.*)—After.
Doppler effect (acoustics)—The observer's sense of pitch depends on the number of pulses which reach him per second, and if this number is artificially increased over the number actually produced per second, he will hear a higher tone. If the source recedes from the observer, or the observer from the source, or both from each other, the pitch will appear to be lowered
Doppio (*It.*)—Double, twofold; sometimes with the octave added.
Dorian mode (*See Mode*)—Similar to the natural minor except that its sixth is raised.
Dorian scale—(*See Table X.*)
Dot—Used after a note to indicate augmentation of its value by one-half; above a note to indicate staccato. (*See Table XIII.*)
Double (*Fr.*)—A previously used term for a variation.
Double-bar—Two vertical lines drawn through the staff at the end of a section, movement or piece.
Double bass—The largest and deepest-toned instrument played with a bow.
Double counterpoint—(*See Invertible counterpoint.*)
Double dot—Appearing to the right of a note or a rest indicates that the note or rest is given one and one-half its original value. (*See Table XIII.*)

Double flat—The symbol (♭♭) placed before the head of a note lowers its pitch two half-steps.
Double fugue—One with two themes.
Double harmonic scale—(*See Table X.*)
Double note—A breve. (*See Table III.*)
Double octave—The interval of two octaves. A fifteenth.
Double pedal point—Occurs when both the tonic and dominant tones are held together.
Double period (*See Period*)—Grouping of two periods.
Double quartet—A quartet for two sets of four solo voices, or of four solo instruments.
Double reed—The vibrating reed of instruments of the oboe class.
Double sharp—The notation (𝄪) placed before the head of a note raises its pitch two half-steps.
Double-stop—The execution of two simultaneous notes on the violin or other string instrument.
Double time—A time in which every measure is composed of two equal parts.
Doubling—Occurs when a tone of a chord sounds simultaneously in another voice, either at the unison or octave.
Doubly-augmented interval—An interval 1/2 tone higher or greater than the regular augmented interval. (*See Table VIII.*)
Doubly-diminished interval—An interval 1/2 tone smaller than the regular diminished interval. (*See Table VIII.*)
Doucement (*Fr.*)—Sweetly, softly.
Douleur (*Fr.*)—Grief.
Doux (*Fr.*)—Sweet, soft.
Down-beat—The interval pulse of a measure of music.
Down bow sign—A sign used in string music indicating that the bow is to be drawn down. (*See Table XIII.*)
Doxology—A hymn or song of praise.
Dreifach (*Ger.*)—Divided in three parts.
Dritta (*It.*), **Dritto** (*It.*)—Right; mano dritta, the right hand.
Droit (*Fr.*)—Right, right hand.
Drum—An instrument of percussion, having heads of vellum or parchment at each end.
D. S.—(*See Dal Segno.*)
Du talon (*Fr.*)—At the frog.
Duet, Duo (*Fr.*), **Duetto** (*It.*)—A composition for two voices or instruments or for two performers upon one instrument.
Duo, due (*It.*)—Two.
Duodecad—Twelve-note chord.
Duodecuple meter—Term used to describe any meter containing twelve beats to a measure.
Duolo (*It.*)—Grief, sorrow.
Duple—Double. Duple time, two beats in the measure. (*See Table IV.*)
Duple meter—Regular grouping to time units by two.
Duplet—A group of two notes to be played in the time of three.
Dur (*Ger.*)—Major, major key.
Duration—A relative length of a tone or rest.
Durational accent—In a series of tones of unequal duration, tones longer than their immediate neighbors tend to accumulate stress. Also Agogic Accent.
Dynamics—Varying and contrasting degrees of intensity or loudness.

Dynamic accentuation—Pertaining to one individual note rather than a group of notes.
Dynamic indications—Directions for nuances of loud and soft, such as crescendi, diminuendi and sforzandi. These are not terms relative to elements of harmonic rhythm, but are used to confirm the natural rhythmic feeling already present in music.

— E —

E—The third note of the scale of C major. In Italian, e or ed means "and."
Ecclesiastical modes—Octave scales used in medieval church music. (*See Table X.*)
Echapee—A non-harmonic tone which is usually approached from a harmonic tone one scale step below, and then leaps downward to a harmonic tone. (*See Table XI.*)
Echo—A sound produced by reverberation—an echo organ stop.
Eco (*It.*)—Echo.
Écossais (*Fr.*)—Scottish, in Scottish style.
E dur (*Ger.*)—Key of E major.
Ed (*It.*)—And.
Eddies (acoustics)—Movement formed by moving air when it passes around a pole or wire.
Edge tone—Produced when a stream of air passes rapidly over an edge at a certain critical angle as in a flute.
Egualmente—Equally; steadily.
Eight—An octave.
Eighth-note (quaver)—A unit of music notation which receives one-half the time value of a quarter note. (*See Table III.*)
Eight-tone Spanish scale—(*See Table X.*)
Einfach (*Ger.*)—Simple, plain.
Einleitung (*Ger.*)—Leading in; introductory.
Eis (*Ger.*)—E sharp.
Electronic music—Music which is produced on electronic instruments such as the Theramin or Ondes Martinot which are "played" by moving the hands towards or away from a sensitive tube. The term also includes electric instruments that simulate the sound of the organ, guitar, or other conventional instruments. Used more precisely, the term *electronic music* has nothing to do with synthetic instruments. It refers to a kind of music which originated in the Studio for Electronic Music of the West German Radio, in Cologne, and its sound material is produced by electronic devices, recorded on magnetic tape, and heard through loudspeakers.
Eleganza (*It.*)—Elegance, grace.
Elegy—A composition of a mournful and commemorative character.
Eleventh—An interval comprised of an octave and a fourth. (*See Table VIII.*)
Elision—(1) Form: an omission of one or more measures between phrases. (2) Harmony: an omission of one or more chords in the order of normal progression.
Embellishment—Same as coloratura, ornamentation, etc.
Embouchure (*Fr.*)—(1) The mouthpiece of a wind instrument; (2) The position and management of the mouth and lips of the player.
E moll (*Ger.*)—Key of E minor. The relative minor of G major.
Empfindung (*Ger.*)—Feeling, emotion, sensitiveness.

En allant (*Fr.*)—Moving, flowing.
Energico (*It.*)—Energetic, forcible.
Enfatico (*It.*)—Emphatical; with earnestness.
English fingering—When the sign (x) is used to designate the thumb it is called English fingering. When the thumb is considered as the first finger (1), it is called German fingering, erroneously called American fingering.
Englisch horn (*Ger.*)—English horn.
Enharmonic—The same pitch given two different letter names in the equal tempered scale.
Enharmonic chords—Chords which have different notation but the same sound. Ex.: C-E-G, B♯-Dx-Fx, etc.
Enharmonic interval—An interval formed between two enharmonic tones.
Enharmonic modulation—An enharmonic modulation occurs when there has been an enharmonic change (either actual or implied) at the point of modulation.
Enharmonic tones—Tones which have different notation but the same sound. Ex.: F♯, G flat; B♯, C; etc.
Enigma canon—A type of canon popular before J. S. Bach. Also called the Puzzle canon and the Riddle canon.
Enigmatic scale—(*See Table X.*)
Enlevez les sourdines (*Fr.*)—Take off mutes.
Ensemble (*Fr.*)—Unity, smoothness; literally "togetherness." A piece for several performers.
Entr'acte (*Fr.*)—Music played between the acts.
Episode—A middle or intermediate section. A digression from the principal theme in the fugue.
Equal counterpoint—Counterpoint in equal notes.
Equal duration—Units divided into two, three or four equal parts, creating regular groups of two, three and four.
Equal temperament (acoustics)—A system of tuning whereby the octave is divided into twelve equal semitones.
Equivocal chord—A dissonant chord of uncertain resolution.
Erhaben (*Ger.*)—Lofty, elevated.
Ernst (*Ger.*)—Earnest; serious.
Eroica (*It.*)—Heroic.
Erotik (*Ger.*)—A love song; an amorous composition.
Es (*Ger.*)—E-flat.
Escape tone—A non-harmonic tone derived step-wise leaping to a harmonic tone. (*See Table XI.*)
Es dur (*Ger.*)—E flat major.
Es moll (*Ger.*)—E flat minor.
Espressione (*It.*)—With expression.
Espressivo (*It.*)—Expressive; with expression.
Essential—A sharp or flat in a key signature.
Essential tones—Tones which form the accepted harmonic elements of any period of writing.
Et (*Fr.*) (*Lat.*)—And.
Ethnomusicology—Presently the accepted term for what was previously known as comparative musicology. The latter name derives from the fact that the approach to the study of music of various peoples was in the earlier days of the field mainly comparative. This approach has now been largely discarded in favor of investigating each musical culture in terms of its own society and geographical area.

Etta, etto (*It.*)—Diminutive terminations.
Étude (*Fr.*)—A study or exercise with some particular technical problem stressed.
Etwas (*Ger.*)—Somewhat; some; a little.
Evaporation—A dissonant tone may evaporate by skipping to another member of the same chord or may freeze in parallel harmony and not resolve until the end of the passage.
Exposition—The initial section of musical forms which contains the thematic material.
Expressif (*Fr.*)—Expressive.
Expression—Represents that part of music which cannot be indicated by notes or by any symbol or sign whatsoever.
Extended compass—Tones beyond the usual range. (*See Tables XVI, XVII and XVIII.*)
Extended groups—Irregular groups of two, three or four tones, the total duration of which is greater than one time unit.
Extensity—Gives a relative feeling of small to big.
Extreme interval—Usually referring to an augmented interval.

— F —

F—The fourth note of the scale of C major. Abbreviation for forte.
F clef—Clef which locates small f on the five-line staff. (*See Table VII.*)
Fa (*It.*)—The name applied to the fourth degree of the scale. In the "fixed" Do system, it is always F.
Facile (*It.*)—Light, easy.
Fa dièse (*Fr.*)—F sharp.
Fagott (*Ger.*)—Bassoon.
Fagotto (*It.*)—Bassoon.
False entries—Passages which suggest the subject of a fugue, and then depart from it.
False modulation—The effect of changing tonality without actually leaving the original key.
False relation—The chromatic contradiction of a tone in one part by another part, by a tone and its chromatically altered octave, either simultaneously or consecutively. (*See Cross relation.*)
False sequence—A restatement of a figure which only partially adheres to sequential treatment.
Falsetto—Very high head tones in the male or female voice.
Fandango (*Sp.*)—A lively dance in triple meter.
Fanfare—A flourish of trumpets or trumpet call.
Fantasie—A composition free in form—an improvisation.
Fantastico (*It.*), **Fantastique** (*Fr.*)—Fantastic; grotesque.
F dur (*Ger.*)—Key of F major.
Feierlich (*Ger.*)—Festal; pompously.
Feminine ending—One which closes on a metrically weak beat.
Fermata (*It.*)—A hold or pause. (*See Table XIII.*)
Feroce (*It.*)—Wild; fierce.
Fervente (*It.*), **Fervore, con** (*It.*)—Fervently, ardently, passionately.
Fes (*Ger.*)—F-flat.
Feurig (*Ger.*)—Fiery; ardent.
Fife—A small, shrill musical instrument of the flute type.

Fifteenth—A double octave. Also an organ stop of two-foot pitch.
Fifth—The fifth degree of the diatonic scale. An interval of five diatonic steps. (*See Table VII.*)
Fifth, hidden—A fifth which is reached, not in parallel, but in similar motion.
Figuration—Type of accompaniment in which the harmony is set in the manner of broken chords, arpeggios, etc.
Figure—A small grouping of notes capable of being identified as a basis from which the phrase is created.
Figured—Provided with figures, as figured bass.
Figured bass—A system of musical shorthand whereby chords are indicated by figures placed below the bass line.
Filar la voce (*It.*)—To spin out or prolong a tone with the voice; to let the tone diminish very gradually.
Finale (*It.*)—The closing piece. The last movement in a symphony or sonata.
Fine (*It.*)—The end. The term used to indicate the end of a composition.
Fingering—The act of placing and using the fingers properly in performing upon a musical instrument; the figures written in music to show the performer which finger to use.
Fino (*It.*)—Until, as far as, up to.
Fioriture (*It.*)—Embellishments in singing.
First—Prime or unison interval. (*See Table VIII.*)
First classification chord—A dominant function chord; chords built on either the dominant or leading tone progressing normally to the tonic.

First inversion chord—Occurs when the third of the triad is placed in the bass or lowest voice.

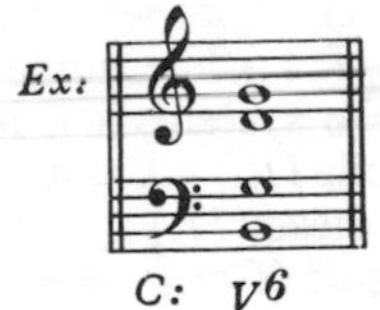

First inversion seventh chord—Occurs when the third of the seventh chord is placed in the bass or lowest voice.

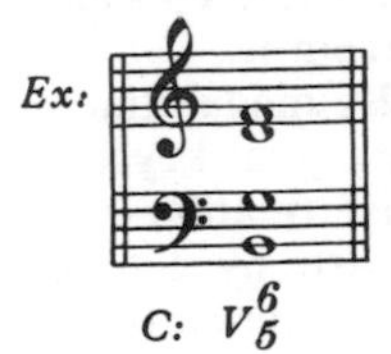

First-Movement form—Sonata Allegro form.
Fis (*Ger.*)—F-sharp.
Fis dur (*Ger.*)—The key of F sharp major.
Fis moll (*Ger.*)—The key of F sharp minor.
Five-three chord—A triad with root as the bass so-called because in figured bass it is indicated by the figures $\frac{5}{3}$ (third and fifth above the bass).
Fixed Do—The system in which Do is always C, as opposed to the moveable Do system in which Do represents the tonic or key note.
Flag—A symbol attached to the right side of the stem of a note to halve its value.
Flageolet—A small pipe, resembling a straight flute, producing a shrill sound.
Flat—The symbol (♭) placed before the head of a note which lowers its pitch one-half tone.
Flauto (*It.*)—Flute.
Flauto Piccolo (*It.*)—Piccolo.

Flöte (*Ger.*)—Flute.
Flute (*Fr.*)—Flute.
F moll (*Ger.*)—Key of F minor.
Folia—A Spanish dance similar to the Fandango.
Foot—Music is similar to poetry, in which the regular pulsations of small groups of syllables, each which is called a foot, must be grouped into the larger units of the verse and the stanza to become artistically useful. Also, as in four-foot, eight-foot organ pipes a measure of pitch.
Force (*Fr.*)—Strength, force.
Foreign chords or tones—Chords or tones which do not belong to a given key or chord.
Foreign modulation—Occurs when the new key's signature differs from that of the original key by more than one accidental.
Foreign progression—A progression in which the two chords involved have no tones in common.
Foreign tonalities—Foreign tonalities differ by more than one accidental.
Form—The organization of all elements of a composition to achieve a certain aesthetic logic.
Formant (acoustics)—The formant theory states that the characteristic tone quality of an instrument is due to the relative strengthening of whatever partial lies with a fixed or relatively fixed region of the musical scale. This region is called a formant of the tone.
Forte (*It.*)—Loud, strong. Abbreviated to F.
Fortissimo (*It.*)—Very loud. Abbreviated to FF.
Forza (*It.*)—Force, power.
Forzando (*It.*)—Forced, accented. (*See Sforzando.*)
Four-part writing—A harmonic concept of writing music; widely used in the 18th and 19th centuries. The term implies, vertically, four factors in each chord, and, horizontally, four different melodic lines.
Fourth—The fourth degree of the diatonic scale; an interval of four diatonic steps. (*See Table VIII.*)
Fourth classification chords—Chords which have their roots on the mediant.
Française (*Fr.*)—A dance in triple meter, resembling the country dance.
Free anticipation—Leaving the anticipation tone by leap.
Free composition—In a free style.
Free counterpoint—Counterpoint in which the melodic lines do not seem to be related to a common harmony.
Free fugue—A fugue written without regard for strict rules.
Free part—A part added to a contrapuntal work to complete the harmony.
Free tone—A non-harmonic tone which is approached and departs by leap. (*See Table XI.*)

French sixth chord—A sixth chord which employs the use of the augmented six-four-three chordal arrangement.

Frequency (acoustics)—The number of cycles of sound waves which occur each second in producing sound. Frequency determines pitch.
Frets—Small strips of wood, ivory or metal, placed upon the fingerboard of certain stringed instruments, to regulate the pitch of the notes produced.
Freudig (*Ger.*)—Joyfully.

Frisch (*Ger.*)—Fresh, lively.
Fröhlich (*Ger.*)—Joyous, gay.
Frozen tones—Accessory tones which have become accepted as chord members, thereby disregarding their previous resolutions.
Frühlingslied (*Ger.*)—Spring song.
F-schlüssel (*Ger.*)—The F or bass clef.
Fugata (*It.*)—The exposition of a fugue.
Fugato (*It.*)—A passage treated in fugal style.
Fughetta (*It.*)—A short fugue.
Fugue—The most mature form of imitative counter-point.
Full cadence (complete)—The cadence progression from tonic to subdominant, to dominant, to tonic. (*See Cadence.*)
Fundamental (acoustics)—The basic or most pronounced tone which generates the overtones.
Fundamental bass—The succession of roots in the harmonic progression.

Fundamental position of triads—Occurs when the root of a triad is in the bass, fifth is in the soprano, and the third is in between.

Funèbre (*Fr.*), **Funebre** (*It.*), **Funerale** (*It.*)—Funereal, mournful.
Fuoco (*It.*)—Fire, passion.
Furioso (*It.*)—Furious, vehement.
Furore (*It.*)—Fury, passion.
Fused compound harmony—A special category of compound chords stems from the triad with added seconds placed in the bass. When formations from this hybrid category are written in open position a unique type of fused, compound harmony is produced. It is possible to fuse two triads so that a single chord of mixed intervals results.
Fz—Abbreviation for forzando.

— G —

G—Fifth note of the scale of C major. Abbreviation for gauche.
G clef—Another term for treble clef; locates g[1] on the five-line staff. (*See Table VII.*)
Gagliarda (*It.*), **Gagliarde** (*Ger.*)—A galliard, an ancient dance.
Gai (*Fr.*)—Gay.
Gaio (*It.*)—Gay.
Gala, di (*It.*)—Gaily, merrily.
Galop (*Fr.*)—A lively round-dance in duple meter.
Gamme (*Fr.*)—A scale.
Gamut (*Ger.*)—Literally " a ladder." A range for certain voices.
Gapped scale—Term used to describe the pentatonic scale.
Gauche (*Fr.*)—Left, left-hand.
Gavotte (*Fr.*)—A French dance usually in common time, strongly accented beginning on the third beat.
G dur (*Ger.*)—Key of G major.
Gebrauchsmusik (*Ger.*)—Everyday music, useful music, functional music.
Gebunden (*Ger.*)—Tied; legato.

Gedehnt (*Ger.*)—Extended, sustained.
Gefühl (*Ger.*)—Feeling, sentiment, expression.
Gehend (*Ger.*)—The same as andante; literally, " going."
Geige (*Ger.*)—The violin.
Geist (*Ger.*)—Spirit, genius, soul.
Gemütlich (*Ger.*)—Easily and cheerily.
Generalbass (*Ger.*)—Thorough bass.
Gentile (*It.*)—Graceful, elegant.

German sixth chord—A sixth chord that uses the augmented six-five-three chordal arrangement.

Ges (*Ger.*)—G-flat.
Ges dur (*Ger.*)—Key of G flat major.
Gestopft (*Ger.*)—Stopped horn.
Gestossen (*Ger.*)—Staccato.
Geteilt (*Ger.*)—Divided.
Getragen (*Ger.*)—Sustained, sostenuto.
Gewöhnlich (*Ger.*)—In the ordinary way.
Gigue (*Fr.*)—A very fast dance of English origin in triple meter.
Giocondo (*It.*)—Cheerful, merry.
Giocoso (*It.*)—Merry, humorous.
Giojoso (*It.*)—Blithe, joyful, gay.
Gioviale (*It.*)—Jovial.
Gis (*Ger.*)—G-sharp.
Gis moll (*Ger.*)—The key of G sharp minor.
Gitana (*It.*)—A Spanish dance.
Giubiloso (*It.*)—Jubilant, exulting.
Giustezza (*It.*)—Precision.
Giusto (*It.*)—Exact, in exact time; moderate, not excessive.
Glee—In England, a secular composition for three or more unaccompanied solo voices.
Glide—Portamento.
Glissando (*It.*)—Gliding; sliding toward a tone instead of attacking it directly. In piano music a scale played by dragging a finger or thumb along the key.
Glocken (*Ger.*)—Bells or chimes.
Glockenspiel (*Ger.*)—Glockenspiel.
Gloria (*Lat.*)—A movement of the Mass.
G moll (*Ger.*)—Key of G minor.
Gondellied (*Ger.*), **-Gondoliera** (*It.*)—A boat song.
Grace note—A note of very short duration, which, in modern usage, take some of the value of the preceding note. (*See Table XII.*)
Gracieux (*Fr.*)—Graceful.
Gracile (*It.*)—Small, thin.
Gradual—A part of the Roman Catholic Mass—a book of chants—an antiphon following the Epistle.
Gran Casa (*It.*)—Bass drum.
Grand (*Fr.*), **Grande** (*It.*)—Large, great, full, complete.
Grandioso (*It.*)—Grand, noble.
Grave (*It.*)—The slowest musical tempo; very slow and solemn.

Grave form—The form of the minor scale in which the sixth and seventh scale degrees are unaltered. (*See Table X.*)
Gravita (*It.*)—Gravity, dignity.
Grazia (*It.*)—Grace, elegance.
Great Octave—Notes lying between C and B inclusive.
Great organ—The chief manual of an organ, and the pipes controlled by it.
Great staff—A combination of treble and bass staves, used in compositions for Piano, Harp, Organ, Celesta, etc.
Gregorian chant—The liturgical chant of the Roman Catholic church; the earliest form of Christian church music.
Grosse Caisse (*Fr.*)—Bass Drum.
Grosse Trommel (*Ger.*)—Bass Drum.
Grosso (*It.*)—Great, grand; full.
Grottesco (*It.*)—Grotesque, comic.
Ground bass—A basso ostinato. A continually repeated bass phrase.
Group—A series of notes of small time value, grouped together; a division or run; a method of setting out band parts in score.
Group fugue—One which consists of a series of fughettas based on different subjects.
Gruppetto (*It.*)—A trill or a turn or any group of grace notes. (*See Table XII.*)
G String—The name of the first string on the double bass, the third on the violoncello, viola and guitar, and the fourth on the violin.
Guaracha (*Sp.*)—Lively Spanish dance.
Guerriero (*It.*)—Martial, war-like.
Guitar—A plucked string instrument.
Gusto (*It.*)—Taste, expression.
Gypsy scale—Harmonic minor scale with the fourth degree raised. The scale contains two augmented seconds, 3-4 and 6-7. (*See Table X.*)

— H —

H—The German B-natural. Heel in organ pedaling.
Habanera (*Sp.*)—A typical Cuban contradance.
Half cadence (*See Cadence*)—The progression of tonic to dominant at the close of a phrase.
Half diminished seventh chord—A chord comprised of a minor third, diminished fifth, and minor seventh. (*See Table XIV.*)
Half note—The second largest unit in modern music notation. The half-note receives half the value of a whole note. (*See Table III.*)
Half rest—A rest the duration of a half-note. (*See Table III.*)
Half-step—Located on the piano keyboard by progressing up and down from any black or white key to the nearest black or white key.
Hallelujah—An invitation to praise, used in every Christian community.
Harfe (*Ger.*)—Harp.
Harmonic (acoustics)—Pertaining to music theory and harmony. One of the "partial tones" generated by the prime tone or fundamental.
Harmonica—The modern mouth harmonica; is a small reed instrument.
Harmonic analysis—The study of harmony dealing with the variants of fundamental structure in harmony.
Harmonic background—Harmony upon which melody is based.
Harmonic dictation—The process of identifying the functions of a tonality when music is played.

Harmonic flute—An open metal organ-stop, of eight- or four-foot pitch.

Harmonic interval—Occurs when two tones of an interval are sounded simultaneously.

Harmonic minor scale—The harmonic minor scale differs from the natural or pure minor scale in that the seventh degree is raised one-half step. (*See Table X.*)

Harmonic modulation—A change in the harmony from one key to another.

Harmonics—Overtones. (*See Table II.*)

Harmonic partials (acoustics)—*See Overtones.*

Harmonic points—The fundamental, third and fifth of a chord.

Harmonic rhythm—An adjustment of the number of chords used in harmonization to the tempo of the melody being harmonized. Related to meter and duration of harmonies.

Harmonic scale—Constructed by arranging in order of ascending or descending pitches all the tones of the key taken from the tonic, subdominant and dominant triads.

Harmonic scale—The scale formed by a series of natural harmonies. (*See Table X.*)

Harmonic series (acoustics)—The tones generated above a fundamental tone by secondary vibrations of the main wave. (*See Table II.*)

Harmonic synthesis—Contemporary harmonic writing is often a composite process which may involve varying placement of the norm of dissonance, choice of a single harmonic idiom or the coalition of one with another, fusion of tonalities, singleness of sound organization or the juxtaposition of tonal and atonal aspects.

Harmonic tetrachord—A tetrachord which consists of a minor second, an augmented second and a minor second.

Harmonic theory (acoustics)—The harmonic theory states that the characteristic tone quality of an instrument is due entirely to the relationship among fundamental and upper partials, which relationship is supposed to remain unchanged no matter what the fundamental is.

Harmonic tone (*See Essential tone*)—A member of a chord.

Harmonium—A small reed-organ.

Harmonization—The process of supplying the harmony to a given melody, or to any given part.

Harmony—The agreement or consonance of sounds uniting into a pleasing whole. The science and study of chords. The simultaneous sound of three or more tones.

Harmony, close—A harmony whose tones are compact, the upper three voices lying within the compass of an octave.

Harmony, dispersed—A harmony in which the notes forming the different chords are separated by wide intervals.

Harpe (*Fr.*)—Harp.

Harpsichord—A keyboard instrument in which the strings are plucked by quills or bits of hard leather. A predecessor to the piano.

Hautbois (*Fr.*)—Oboe.

Havanaise (*Fr.*)—A Habanera.

H dur (*Ger.*)—Key of B major.

H moll (*Ger.*)—The key of B minor.

Head—The round part of the note.

Head register—Utilized by female singers and corresponds in some respects to the usually undeveloped " falsetto " in men.

Head-tones, Head-voice—The vocal tones of the head-register.

Heftig (*Ger.*)—Insistent, boisterous, vehement.
Heimlich (*Ger.*)—Secret, mysterious.
Heiter (*Ger.*)—Serene, cheerful.
Helicon—A brass wind-instrument.
Helmholtz resonator (acoustics)—A spherical shell of metal or glass enclosing a body of air tuned to a certain pitch, and having an aperture for the sound to enter, and another smaller aperture in a protuberance which fits into the ear.
Hemidemisemiquaver—A sixty-fourth note.
Heptad—Seven-note chord.
Hervortretend (*Ger.*)—Prominently.
Herzlich (*Ger.*)—Tenderly, heartfelt.
Heterophony—The duplication of a melody at any interval. A characteristic of primitive music.
Hexachord—A group of six diatonic tones with a semi-tone interval in the middle.
Hexad—Six-note chord.
Hidden octave—Similar motion of outer voices to an octave in a chord progression.
High Mass—The Mass celebrated in the Roman Catholic churches.
Hirajoshi scale—(*See Table X.*)
Hirtlich (*Ger.*)—Pastoral, rustic.
His (*Ger.*)—The note B sharp.
Hoboe (*Ger.*)—Oboe.
Hochzeits-lied (*Ger.*)—Wedding-song.
Hold—A pause or fermata. (*See Table XIII.*)
Holding-note—A note sustained in one voice while the other voices are in motion.
Homophonic—Music in which one voice leads melodically being supported in chordal or a more elaborate manner; melody plus accompaniment.
Homophony—In modern music, a style of melody supported by chords, in contrast to polyphony, which is melody supported by other melodies or parts or voices.
Hook—The curved line attached to the stem of a note. (*See Flag.*)
Horn (*Ger.*)—Horn.
Hornpipe—An old English dance in lively tempo.
Hungarian major scale—(*See Table X.*)
Hungarian minor scale—(*See Gapped scale*). (*See Table X.*)
Hurdy-gurdy—Instrument of ancient origin, consisting of a flat oblong sounding board upon which are stretched four gut strings.
Hurry—Theatrical or stage name for a tremulo passage on the violin or roll on a drum. The " hurry " is generally played as a preparation for the culminating point of a dramatic incident.
Huyghens' principle (acoustics)—The Dutch astronomer Huyghens states that any point on a wave front may become the origin of a secondary series of waves, which diverge in spheres.
Hybrid-type chord—A chord whose function is not limited to any particular group or classification.
Hymn—A religious or sacred song.
Hymnal—Hymn-book; a collection of hymns.
Hypo modes—Plagal church modes which are located a fourth lower than their respective authentic modes. Ex: Hypodorian, hypophrygian, etc.

— I —

I (*It.*)—The.
Iambic—A metrical foot with one short and one long syllable.
Iambus—A metrical foot of two syllables, one short and one long, with the accent on the long.
Idiom—A fragment or portion of music which is indicative of a style or period of music composition. Devices characteristically associated with certain instruments.
Idyl—A short poem in pastoral style.
Il (*It.*)—The.
Il fine (*It.*)—The end.
Imagists—A name given to composers who avoid rhetoric, preconceived patterns, and the elaborate structures of the 19th century, and to intimate by imagery rather than to describe concretely and directly.
Imitation—Repetition of a theme, motive or phrase introduced by one part, the antecedent, in another part, the consequent. An essential element of contrapuntal style.
Immer (*Ger.*)—Always, ever.
Imperfect authentic cadence—An authentic cadence which has the third or fifth in the soprano of the tonic triad.
Imperfect plagal cadence—A plagal cadence in which the soprano note is changed in the progression IV-I.
Impetuoso (*It.*)—Impetuous, hasty.
Implied modulation—A modulation in which there is no accidental to indicate the change of tonality.
Impresario (*It.*)—A conductor or manager of a concert or opera organizatio
Impromptu (*Fr.*)—A piece of an extemporaneous character.
Improvization (Extemporization)—The art of musical performance without aid of memorization or notation.
Improvize—To create spontaneously.
Impulse, melodic—A point in a melodic line where a certain stress is felt in the notes written.
Im Zeitmass (*Ger.*)—In the original speed.
Incalzando (*It.*)—To chase.
Incidental music—Music written to go with a play or drama.
Incomplete cadence—Occurs when some tone other than the key-note is in the soprano of the tonic chord.
Incomplete chord—A chord with one or more of its members omitted.
Indeciso (*It.*)—In an undecided manner.
Inferior relative triad—A triad which is lower in pitch than the one which it is related to.
Infinite canon—One without a closing cadence.
Inharmonic partial (acoustics)—Occurs when an upper partial has a frequency greater than five times the fundamental frequency but less than six times.
Inharmonic tones (*See Non-harmonic tones*)—Tones which do not fit in the chord structure. (*See Table XI.*)
Inner parts—The alto and tenor voices. Parts in the harmonic structure lying between the highest and lowest.
Innig (*Ger.*)—Deep, sincere, earnest.
Innocente (*It.*)—Unaffected, artless.
Inquieto (*It.*)—Unrestful, uneasy.
Instantemente (*It.*)—Urgently.
Instrument—Any mechanical contrivance for the production of sound.

Instrumentation—The theory and practice of composing, arranging, or adapting music for a group of instruments of different kinds.
In tempo (*It.*)—In strict time.
Intensity—A relative feeling of soft to loud.
Intenzione, con (*It.*)—Stress, emphasis.
Interference (acoustics)—Particles which make up the medium will tend to group themselves into points of much agitation and points of rest.
Interlude—A passage connecting the main sections of a composition.
Intermezzo—Incidental music; a short movement interpolated between the main sections of a work.
Interval—The pitch relation or distance between two tones. Interval types are: Major, minor, perfect, augmented, diminished. (*See Table VIII.*)
Interval, dissonant—An interval which sounds restless and needs resolution.
Interval, enharmonic—Two or more intervals that sound the same when played, but have different meanings. Ex.: Augmented second and minor third.

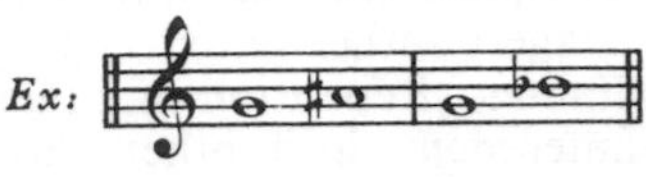

Intimo (*It.*)—Heartfelt. Inward emotion.
Intonation—Formerly. The production of a tone. In modern usage intonation denotes the singing or playing in tune.
Intoning—The practice of chanting in the Anglican church service.
Intrepido (*It.*)—Intrepid, bold.
Introduction—A phrase or division preparatory to a composition or major section of a composition.
Introit—An antiphon sung while the priest proceeds to the altar to celebrate Mass. In the Anglican church, a short anthem or hymn sung as the minister approaches the communion table.
Invention—A short piece in free contrapuntal style.
Inversion—A change of an octave in the pitch of one or more notes in an interval or chord; such chords where the bass tone is other than the root. The first inversion of a triad appears with the third in the bass and the second inversion with the fifth, etc.
Invertible scales—Scales which are naturally reflective in that two separate scales move identically, interval for interval, when placed in contrary motion. The entire diatonic scale system is symmetrically invertible.
Involution—The projection down from the lowest tone of a given chord, using the same intervals in the order of their occurrence in the given chord, we refer to as involution.
Ionian mode—Same as the major mode of today. (*See Table X.*)
Irato (*It.*)—Wrathfully.
Irregular duration—Occurs when durations of component sounds are unequal.
Irregular meters—Meters which deviate from the normal bipartite and tripartite metrical schemes.
Irregular syncopation—Occurs when the duration of two tones which are tied together is unequal.
Irlandais (*Fr.*)—In the Irish style.
Ironico (*It.*)—Ironical.
Irresoluto (*It.*)—Irresolute, undecided.
Isomelos—In isorhythm, the pitch levels are free and used with a repeated rhythmic pattern, but when the rhythm is free with a repeated melodic pattern, a device called isomelos exists.
Isorhythm—When one or more voices of changing notes adhere to a single rhythmic pattern, isorhythm exists.

Issimo (*It.*)—A superlative termination.
Istesso (*It.*)—The same.
Italiano (*It.*)—In the Italian style.

Italian sixth chord—An augmented sixth chord.

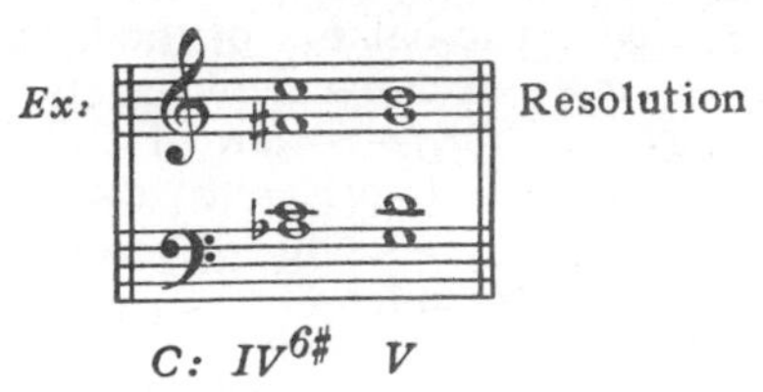

Ite missa est (*Lat.*)—The concluding words of the Mass.

— J —

Jack—The quill or hopper which strikes the strings of a harpsichord, or the upright lever in piano action.
Jagd-stück (*Ger.*)—A hunting piece.
Janko keyboard—A system of piano keys in several manuals, or ranks, invented by Paul von Janko. This keyboard necessitates only a small stretch for large intervals.
Jazz—A significant musical art form which has been created and developed almost solely in America and is characterized by a great degree of skilful improvisation, distinct rhythmic punctuation, and an original approach to instrumentation and orchestration.
Jeu (*Fr.*)—Play; also a stop on the organ.
Jeu de timbres (*Fr.*)—Glockenspiel.
Jig. Gigue (*Fr.*), **Giga** (*It.*)—A lively dance.
Jodeln (*Ger.*)—A style of singing peculiar to the Tyrolese and Swiss.
Jota (*Sp.*)—A Spanish national dance.
Jubel-lied (*Ger.*)—Song of jubilee.
Jubilate—In the Anglican liturgy, the one hundredth psalm.
Jubiloso (*It.*)—Jubilant, exulting.
Just intonation—The correct sounding of intervals in singing or playing.
Juxtaposition of keys—A change of key without any modulatory process whatever.

— K —

Kammer (*Ger.*)—Chamber.
Kanon (*Ger.*)—A canon.
Kapelle (*Ger.*)—Chapel.
Kapellmeister (*Ger.*)—The director of music, in church, chorus or orchestra.
Kastagnetten (*Ger.*)—Castanets.
Kettledrum—An orchestral drum consisting of a hollow brass or copper shell, over the top of which a head of vellum or plastic is stretched.
Key—A scale, the key being the first (tonic) note of the scale. The beginning key in a piece of music. The ultimate key or ending key in comparison to other keys used in a composition. A lever opening, or closing a hole in wind instruments. The lever that is moved to make the piano action strike the strings.
Keyboard—The whole series of levers for producing tone in a piano, harpsichord, or organ.

Keynote—The first note of a key or scale.
Key relationship—Keys of nearest relationship to a given key are those having one sharp (or flat) more or less in the signature.
Key scheme—The balance of the keys in support of a main tonality.
Key signature—A convenient grouping of accidentals used in a piece.
Kinderscenen (*Ger.*)—Scenes of childhood; a name given by Schumann to a collection of little pieces for the piano.
Kinderstück (*Ger.*)—Child's piece.
Klang (*Ger.*)—Sound.
Klarinette (*Ger.*)—Clarinet.
Klavier (*Ger.*)—A keyboard instrument; used to denote harpsichord, clavichord, etc.
Klavierauszug—Piano-forte arrangement.
Kleine Flöte (*Ger.*)—Piccolo.
Kleine Trommel (*Ger.*)—Snare drum.
Knee-stop—A lever controlled by the knees; used on reed organs.
Kontrabass (*Ger.*)—Double Bass.
Kontrafagott (*Ger.*)—Contra Bassoon.
Kraft (*Ger.*)—Force; vigour.
Kräftig (*Ger.*)—Powerful, strong, energetic.
Krakowiak—A Polish dance.
Kreuz (*Ger.*)—The sign of a sharp.
Kumoi scale—(*See Table X.*)
Kurz (*Ger.*)—Short, detached staccato.
Kyrie eleison (*Ger.*)—The first movement in a Mass.

— L —

L—Abbreviation for left, or (*Ger.*) linke, hand.
La (*It.*)—A syllable applied in singing, etc., to the sixth note of the scale. Also refers to the submediant.
La Bémol (*Fr.*)—The note A flat.
La Bémol Majeur (*Fr.*)—The key of A flat major. (*See Table IX.*)
La Bémol Mineur (*Fr.*)—The key of A flat minor. (*See Table IX.*)
La Destra (*It.*)—The right hand.
La Diesè (*Fr.*)—The note A sharp.
Lagrimoso (*It.*)—Mournfully, tearfully.
Lamentoso (*It.*)—Lamenting, mournful.
La Meta (*It.*)—Half a string group.
La Moitié (*Fr.*)—Half a string group.
Lancers—The name of one of the arrangements of sets of country dances.
Landini cadence—Occurs when the upper voice moves from the seventh degree to the tone below, and then leaps to the tonic.
Ländler (*Ger.*)—A country dance in triple meter.
Langsam (*Ger.*)—Slow. The same as lento.
Languendo (*It.*)—Languishing.
Largamente (*It.*)—Broadly, with fullness.
Largando (*It.*)—Gradually slower and broader.
Larghetto (*It.*)—A tempo not quite as slow as largo.
Larghissimo (*It.*)—As slow as possible.
Largo (*It.*)—A slow, broad tempo, almost as slow as grave.
Laryngoscope—An instrument for examining the larynx.

Larynx—The organ of the voice, by which we produce vocal sounds, situated at the top of the wind-pipe.
Launig (*Ger.*)—Humorous, capricious.
Lay—A song, a ballad.
Le (*It.*) (*Fr.*)—The.
Leader—A director or conductor.
Leading-tone—Referring to the seventh degree of the scale. (*See Table X.*)
Leading-tone seventh chord—A seventh chord built on the seventh degree, usually an incomplete dominant ninth, which partakes of non-dominant characteristics when it proceeds to III. (*See Table XIV.*)
Leading tone triad—A triad built on the seventh degree of the scale, rarely found in root position. In its action and effect this triad often functions as an incomplete dominant seventh chord.
Leaning note—Appoggiatura. (*See Table XI.*)
Leap—A skip; any interval larger than a second.
Lebhaft (*Ger.*)—Lively, quick.
Leçon (*Fr.*)—A lesson; an exercise.
Ledger line—Short line used as an extension above and below the regular five-line staff.
Legatissimo (*It.*)—Extremely smooth and fluent.
Legato (*It.*)—Smooth, with no pause between notes.
Légende (*Fr.*)—A legend; a piece written in a romantic style.
Leggieramente (*It.*)—Lightly, swiftly.
Leggiero (*It.*)—Light, delicate.
Leicht (*Ger.*)—Easy, facile.
Leidenschaftlich (*Ger.*)—Passionate.
Leise (*Ger.*)—Low, soft, gentle.
Leitmotiv (*Ger.*)—Leading motive; a compositional device whereby a motive is identified with a specific character, event, etc.
Lentado (*It.*)—With increased slowness.
Lento (*It.*)—A slow tempo, usually between adagio and andante.
Lesser—Minor.
Lesto (*It.*)—Lively, nimbly, gay.
Libretto (*It.*)—The words of an opera or oratorio in book form.
Licenza (*It.*)—License, freedom of style.
Lié (*Fr.*)—Tied, bound.
Lieblich (*Ger.*)—Lovely, charming.
Lied (*Ger.*)—A song; a ballad.
Lieder ohne Worte (*Ger.*)—A short song-like piano piece.
Ligature—Tones of longer duration falling upon time units which are normally weak in the scheme of metric accentuation. The predecessor of the tie used in neumatic notation. Also a metal device used to secure a reed to the mouthpiece of a woodwind instrument.
Ligne (*Fr.*)—A line.
Lilt—An Irish dance accompanied with singing.
Linear motion—Scale-wise motion; step-wise motion.
Linke (*Ger.*)—Left, left-hand.
Listening—Listening in all degrees of intensity, is a neutral activity dependent only in a very general sense upon actual physical hearing. It is a combination of intuition and knowledge. It includes remembering what was heard in the past and anticipating that which is to follow.
L'istesso tempo (*It.*)—In the same tempo as the previous section.
Litany—A song of supplication.

Loco (*It.*)—Place. Used to show a return to the pitch of printed notes after an 8va transposition.
Locrian Mode—Derived from the Aeolian by lowering both the second and the fifth degrees. (*See Table X.*)
Long—Numatic note value equal to two or three breves.
Longitudinal wave (acoustics)—Vibrating particles moving to and fro in the same direction as the wave is traveling.
Lontano (*It.*)—Far away.
Loop (acoustics)—Moving portions of vibrating parts occuring between nodes or points of rest.
Loudness—(*See Volume.*)
Loud pedal—The pianoforte pedal which lifts the dampers; the right pedal.
Loure or louvre (*Fr.*)—A French dance adapted to an air called " L'aimable vainqueur " in 6/4 or 3/4 meter and slow tempo.
Lugubre (*It.*)—Mournful, dismal.
Lunatico (*It.*)—Performed in the spirit of lunacy.
Lunga (*It.*)—Long.
Lusingando (*It.*)—Coaxingly.
Lustig (*Ger.*)—Merry, gay.
Lute—A very ancient stringed instrument of the guitar family.
Luttuoso (*It.*)—Sorrowful, mournful.
Lydian Major scale—(*See Table X.*)
Lydian Minor scale—(*See Table X.*)
Lydian mode—The same as the major except that its fourth degree is raised one semitone. (*See Table X.*)
Lyre—One of the most ancient of stringed instruments, a sort of harp.
Lyric—Poetry or blank verse intended to be set to music.

— M —

M—Abbreviation for mano or main, meaning hand.
M. M.—Abbreviation for Maelzel's metronome.
Ma (*It.*)—But.
Madrigal—A vocal setting of a short lyric poem in three to six contrapuntal parts; usually for unaccompanied chorus.
Maestoso (*It.*)—Majestic, stately.
Maggiore (*It.*)—Major, referring to mode.
Maggot—One of the later names given to fancies, airs and pieces of an impromptu character.
Main (*Fr.*)—Hand.
Mais (*Fr.*)—But.
Majestätisch (*Ger.*)—Majestically.
Major—Greater as opposed to minor, lesser.
Major cadence—A cadence on a major triad.
Major chord—One having a major third and perfect fifth. (*See Table XIV.*)
Major intervals—Major intervals are from the tonic to the second, third, sixth, and seventh degrees as they occur in the major scale. Any minor interval enlarged by one semitone becomes a major interval. (*See Table VIII.*)
Major Locrian scale—(*See Table X.*)
Major mode—Derived from a major scale which has one full or two half-steps between each degree, except between the third and fourth degree and the seventh and octave which have a half-step. (*See Table X.*)

Major scale—Derived from the major mode. (*See Major mode.*)
Major-minor seventh chord (M7)—A seventh chord comprised of a major triad and a major seventh interval above the root. (*See Table XIV.*)
Major-minor seventh chord—A seventh chord comprised of a major triad and a minor seventh interval above the root. (*See Table XIV.*)
Major-minor system—The acknowledged superior authority of major and minor modes over a period of some three hundred years.
Major second—An interval comprised of two semitones. (*See Table VIII.*)
Major seventh—An interval comprised of eleven semitones. (*See Table VIII.*)
Major sixth—An interval comprised of nine semitones. (*See Table VIII.*)
Major tetrachord—A tetrachord that is built with the following intervals between its notes—a major second followed by a major second, followed by a minor second.
Major third—An interval comprised of four semitones. (*See Table VIII.*)
Major triad—A major triad contains a major third and a perfect fifth. (*See Table XIV.*)
Malincolico (*It.*)—Melancholy. In a melancholy style.
Mancando (*It.*)—Decreasing; dying away.
Manche (*Fr.*)—The neck of a violin or guitar.
Mandolin—A small stringed instrument generally almond shaped.
Mandolinata (*It.*)—A mandolin piece of quiet character, like a serenade.
Manica (*It.*)—Fingering.
Maniera (*It.*)—Manner, style, method.
Mano (*It.*)—Hand.
Manual—An organ keyboard.
Marcando (*It.*)—Strongly marked.
Marcato (*It.*)—Marked, accented.
March—A composition with strongly marked rhythm, suitable for accompanying troops in walking. Generally written in 2/4 or 6/8 meter.
Marcia (*It.*)—March.
Marimba—A musical instrument made of a series of graduated pieces of hard wood, which are struck with hammers.
Marionette (*It.*)—A puppet.
Markiert (*Ger.*)—Strongly accented.
Marks of Expression—Words or signs used in music to regulate the degrees of accent, time, or tone, required to produce the artistic effect of a composition. (*See Table XIII.*)
Marseillaise (*Fr.*)—A song written by Rouget de Lisle in 1792, and became the French National Anthem.
Martelé (*Fr.*)—Very strongly accented.
Martellato (*It.*)—Strongly marked.
Marziale (*It.*)—Martial.
Masculine ending—Occurs when the final cadence chord falls on an accented beat; the bar line being placed just before V in the half cadence and before I in the authentic cadence. (*See Cadence.*)
Masque—A musical drama popular in the 16th and 17th centuries.
Mass, Missa (*Lat.*), **Messa** (*It.*), **Messe** (*Fr.*), (*Ger.*)—In the Roman Catholic Church the celebration of the Eucharist of Last Supper. Also celebrated in some High Anglican churches. Portions of the Mass usually set to music, namely the Kyrie, the Gloria, the Credo, the Sanctus and the Agnus Dei.
Massig (*Ger.*)—Moderate, moderato.
Mazurka (*It.*)—A Polish national dance in triple meter.
Meantone tuning (acoustics)—Prior to the middle of the 19th century in England

a compromise tuning which had a widespread vogue was the meantone tuning.

M.D.—Abbreviation of (1) Mano destra or main droite, the right hand; (2) Doctor of Music.

Measure—The space between two bar-lines.

Mediant (Mi) (*See Degree*)—Referring to the third degree of the scale.

Megadizing (acoustics)—The use of the octave in concerted singing.

Meistersänger (*Ger.*)—Master-singers; the successors of the minnesingers or Troubadours.

Melancolia (*It.*)—Melancholy.

Melismatic—The use of many notes for one syllable of text.

Melodeon—The original American reed organs were called Melodeons.

Melodia (*It.*)—Melody.

Melodic dictation—The process of reproducing in musical notation a melody which has been played.

Melodic interval—Occurs when two tones are sounded consecutively.

Melodic minor scale—The melodic minor scale differs from the natural or pure minor scale in that the sixth and seventh degrees are raised one-half step in the ascending scale—the descending melodic and natural minor scales are identical. (*See Table X.*)

Melodic progression—Chord progressions moving with conjunct motion.

Melodic repetition—An exact restatement upon the same scale-steps of a group or figure.

Melodic rhythm—The rhythm of four different voices.

Melodic scales—Constructed by linking together chord tones by means of passing tones.

Melodic sequence—The repetition of a melodic unit whether it be a motive, a half phrase, or a period, on a tonal level higher or lower than the initial unit.

Melodic set—At any point in the formal shape a melodic group of notes may control harmonic texture. Any succession of any number of tones, not necessarily all different, may be used in two or more voices at once, forming harmony from horizontal movement or divided between voices, forming harmony from vertical telescoping.

Melodic skips—Melodic skips are produced when a melody moves by intervals larger than a second.

Melodrama—Originally a musical drama; now a stage-declamation in which the interest is heightened by musical accompaniment.

Melody—An organized succession of three or more tones.

Melody law—The inherent desire of every tone to move to its nearest neighbor in the scale.

Melos (*Gr.*)—Song.

Membranes (acoustics)—Thought of as " two-dimensional strings," in that they must be stretched to secure sufficient elasticity to vibrate. They are usually circular, as in drums, and may vibrate in various forms, depending on how many nodal diameters or circles form.

Meme (*Fr.*)—The same.

Meno (*It.*)—Less.

Meno mosso (*It.*)—Less movement, slower.

Mensurable notation—Notes invented in the 12th century to express exact time values; more commonly, " mensural notation."

Menuet (*Fr.*)—A minuet; a slow dance in 3/4 meter.

Menuetto (*It.*)—Minuet.

Messa (*It.*)—A Mass.

Messa di voce (*It.*)—A gradual swelling and subsiding on a single tone in singing or playing. (*See Table XIII.*)
Mesto (*It.*)—Gloomy; sad.
Mestoso (*It.*)—Sadly.
Mesure (*Fr.*)—Measure. Time.
Meter—The basic scheme of note values and accents which remain unaltered throughout a composition or section thereof. (*See Table IV.*)
Meter signature—A symbol indicating the type of meter and the unit of the beat. (*See Table IV.*)
Method—System of teaching.
Metric accent—An accent which undulates between accented and unaccented beats.
Metronome—An apparatus to indicate the exact tempo of a piece of music. Invented by John Maelzel in 1815, the metronome is a device in which a weighted rod, projected upward, swings from side to side in regular time, to mark the beats of a measure. The rate may be varied by a movement of the weight. Figures are placed on the rod, indicating where the weight should be put to obtain any desired number of beats per minute. Composers sometimes mark their pieces with a metronome mark; i.e., a figure and a note of definite value, showing that the piece must be played so as to sound that number of notes of the given value in a minute.
Mezzo (*It.*)—The middle, half.
Mezzo forte (mf) (*It.*)—Moderately loud.
Mezzo piano (mp) (*It.*)—Moderately soft.
Mezzo-soprano—A voice lower in range than a soprano and higher than a contralto. (*See Table XVI.*)
Mezzo-soprano clef (*See Table VII.*)
Mezzo Voce—Half voice.
M.G.—Abbreviation of " main gauche " (*Fr.*) the left hand.
Mi (*See Degree*)—Referring to the third degree of the scale. A syllable used for the third note of the scale in singing, etc.
Mi bémol (*Fr.*)—The note E flat.
Mi bémol majeur or mineur—The key of E flat major or minor. (*See Table IX.*)
Microtone—An interval smaller than a semitone.
Microtone scales—Scales consisting of more than twelve semi tones to the octave. These scales may involve the use of quarter tones, sixth tones, eighth tones, and even smaller divisions of the octave.
Middle " c "—The " c " near the middle of the keyboard. It is located on the first ledger line above the bass staff and the first ledger line below the treble staff. (*See Table I.*)
Mi dièse (*Fr.*)—The note E sharp.
Minacciando (*It.*)—Threateningly.
Minim—(*See Half-note.*)
Minnesingers (*Ger.*)—German name for poets of the Troubadour character.
Minor (*Lat.*)—Less; smaller.
Minor chord—A chord comprised of a minor third and perfect fifth. (*See Table XIV.*)
Minor chromatic scale—The singing or playing of the twelve semitones within the octave, with underlying minor key construction.
Minor (Harmonic) scale—(*See Table X.*)
Minor intervals—Minor intervals are those from the tonic to the third, sixth and seventh degree as they occur in the natural minor scale. Any major interval made smaller by one semitone becomes a minor interval. (*See Table VIII.*)

Minor-major seventh (mM7)—A chord comprised of a minor triad and a major seventh interval above the root. (*See Table XIV.*)
Minor (Melodic) scale—(*See Table X.*)
Minor-minor seventh or minor seventh (m7)—A chord comprised of a minor triad and a minor seventh interval above the root. (*See Table XIV.*)
Minor mode (*See Mode*)—Basically the same as major, both containing the same tonic, supertonic, subdominant, and dominant degrees. The mediant is lowered one-half step and the sixth and seventh degrees vary with the scale. (*See Pure, Harmonic, and Melodic minor.*) (*See Table X.*)
Minor (Natural Aeolian) scale—(*See Table X.*)
Minor, relative—A minor key which has the same key signature as that of a major key. (*See Table IX.*)
Minor scale (*See Scale*)—Basically the same as minor mode. (*See Minor mode.*) (*See Table X.*)
Minor second—An interval comprised of one semitone. (*See Table VIII.*)
Minor seventh—An interval comprised of ten semitones. (*See Table VIII.*)
Minor sixth—An interval comprised of eight semitones. (*See Table VIII.*)
Minor tetrachord—A tetrachord built with the following intervals between its notes—a major second, followed by a minor second, followed by a major second.
Minor third—An interval comprised of three semitones. (*See Table VIII.*)
Minor triad (*See Triad*)—A triad consisting of a minor third and a perfect fifth. (*See Table XIV.*)
Minore (*It.*)—Minor, referring to mode.
Minuet—An early French dance-form in slow triple meter.
Mirror fugue—The principle of mirror-reflection applied to a melody placed either at end of the melody (retrograde version) or underneath in which an inverted form results.
Miserere—The 51st Psalm sung in the Tenebrae service in the Roman Catholic Church.
Missa (*Lat.*)—A Mass.
Missklang (*Ger.*)—Discord.
Misterioso (*It.*)—Mysteriously.
Misura (*It.*)—A measure, a bar.
Misurato (*It.*)—Measured; in strict time.
Mit (*Ger.*)—With.
Mit Dämpfer (*Ger.*)—Muted.
Mit Holzschlageln (*Ger.*)—With hard sticks.
Mittelstimmen (*Ger.*)—Inner parts.
Mixed meter—Different meters which follow each other in close succession; also referred to as multimeter.
Mixed minor mode—The mode caused by the alteration of the subtonic producing minor tonic and subdominant chords and a major dominant chord.
Mixed scale—A scale which contains elements of both major and minor.
Mixolydian mode (*See Mode*)—The same as the major except that its seventh is lowered one semitone. (*See Table X.*)
Mixolydian scale—(*See Table X.*)
Mixture stops (acoustics)—In the pipe organ, whose tones on the whole are deficient in upper partials, mixture stops are used, which for every key depressed will cause several pipes to sound, tuned to certain of the harmonic partials of the tone.
M.M.—The abbreviation for Maelzel's metronome.
Mock stretto—A stretto in which false entries are involved.

Modality—The choice of tones between which the relationship of tonality exists.
Mode (*See Aeolian, Dorian, Ionian, Lydian, Major, Minor, Mixolydian, Phrygian, etc.*)—A specific selection and arrangement of tones forming the tonal substance of a composition. In early times, the collective name for scales.
Model degree—The mediant and submediant of a tonality. They have little effect on the tonality but suggest the mode.
Mode ordinaire (*Fr.*)—In the ordinary way.
Moderato (*It.*)—Moderate tempo, between andantino and allegretto.
Modes, rhythmic—A 13th century system of rhythmic organization characterized by the consistent repetition of a certain simple rhythmic pattern.
Modified repetition—A repetition retaining the basic characteristics of the first statement of the group or figure; but in the restatement one or more intermediate tones may be added, or certain tones of the first statement may be omitted.
Modified sequence (*See Modified repetition*)—The same as modified repetition except the unit may be transposed.
Modo (*It.*)—Mode.
Modo Ordinario (*It.*)—In the ordinary way.
Modulate—To pass from one key or mode into another.
Modulation—The process of abandoning one tonality and establishing a new one. It is usually affected by a pivot chord which belongs to both the old and new tonalities. (*See Common chord, Chromatic modulation, etc.*)
Modulatory cadences—Authentic cadences played around the circle of major keys, each one establishing a new key.
Moduliren (*Ger.*)—To modulate.
Modus (*Lat.*)—Style of manner.
Moll (*Ger.*)—Minor.
Molle (*Lat.*)—Soft.
Molto (*It.*)—Much; extremely; a great deal.
Momentum (acoustics)—The tendency of a sound to overshoot the rest position, becoming displaced in the other direction.
Monochord—A scientific instrument which is composed of a sound-box over which is stretched a single string. By means of a movable bridge or a group of movable bridges the string may be divided at any point.
Monody—Music for a single voice or unison group; only one note is heard at a time.
Monotone—A single unvaried tone.
Montant (*Fr.*)—Ascending.
Morceau (*Fr.*)—A composition of an unpretending character.
Mordent (*Ger.*)—A musical ornament consisting of the alternation of the written note with the note immediately below it. (*See Table XII.*)
Morendo (*It.*)—Dying away gradually.
Morris Dance—A rustic dance usually performed in spring and summer time.
Morte (*Fr.*)—The death note of any hunted animal sounded upon a bugle.
Mosso (*It.*)—Movement, motion, speed.
Motet—A sacred vocal composition in contrapuntal style performed without accompaniment.
Motion—The progress of two voices. (*See Direct motion, Oblique motion, Contrary motion, Retrograde motion, etc.*)
Motive—The briefest intelligible and self-contained fragment of a musical theme or subject.
Moto (*It.*)—Motion, movement.

Mouthpiece—That part of a wind instrument which is put into the mouth of the performer.

Movable Do—Generally any system of solmization so designed that the syllables can be used in transposition to any key; " Do " remaining as the tonal center, regardless of key.

Movement—The various complete and comparatively independent divisions which form the sonata, symphony, etc.

Multiplication—A rhythmical element which is slower than the beat of the meter.

Munter (*Ger.*)—Lively.

Musette—(1) A small bagpipe; (2) the name of a melody of a soft character written in imitation of bagpipe tunes; (3) an old dance.

Musica (*It.*)—Music.

Musica ficta (*It.*)—A practice of 15th and 16th century musicians whereby certain tones were given chromatic alterations. This device was chiefly used to provide a cadential leading tone and to avoid the tritone, *b-f.*

Musical alphabet—The present system whereby each octave of notes is composed of letters: *a, b, c, d, e, f, g.*

Musical Box—An instrument, the sounds of which are produced by a steel comb having teeth of graduated length.

Musical creativity—The expression of personal feeling through written tonal and rhythmic configurations.

Music reading—The acquisition of musical insight through the development of the ability to think music and to reproduce it.

Musical sound—A sound characterized by definite pitch, intensity and quality. Musical sounds are produced through vibrating strings, vibrating air columns, and vibrating rods, reeds, plates and membranes.

Musique concrète—Music involving the use of natural sounds and noises, e.g., the wind, a motor accelerating, or a door slamming—are recorded on tape and then treated in all the ways tape can be manipulated—played slower (lowering pitch), faster (raising pitch), backwards (reversing the usual attack-diminuendo pattern), or played in combinations of possible treatments. Compositions are then constructed from this palette of sound.

Muta (*It.*)—A direction to a player or a horn, trumpet, or on drums, to change the key of his instrument.

Mutation (*Fr.*), **Mutazione** (*It.*)—Change.

Mute—A small contrivance of wood, metal, ivory or plastic placed on the bridge of a string instrument to dampen the sound. A pear shaped contrivance used as a mute for brass instruments.

Mutig (*Ger.*)—Spirited; bold.

M.V.—Abbreviation of " mezzo voce."

— N —

Nach (*Ger.*)—After.

Nachahmung (*Ger.*)—Imitation.

Nachdruck (*Ger.*)—Emphasis.

Nacht-musik (*Ger.*)—Literally night music; a serenade.

Naked fifth—A harmonic fifth without an added third.

Naked fourth—A harmonic fourth without an added third.

National Air—Music peculiar to, or characteristic of, a particular nation.

Natural (♮)—Indicates that after a sharp or flat, the original basic tone is to be restored.

Natural invertible counterpoint—Counterpoint which is invertible at the octave or its multiples.
Natural keys—Those which have no sharps or flats in the signature. (*See Table IX.*)
Natural minor scale (pure minor)—The natural minor scale differs from the major scale in that the third, sixth and the seventh degrees are lowered one-half step, both ascending and descending. (*See Aeolian Mode.*) (*See Table X.*)
Natural minor form—A scale resulting from the extraction of the tones of the tonic, subdominant and dominant triads, when all are minor.
Natural period (acoustics)—Every material body which can vibrate has a time of vibration most natural to it, dependent on such factors as size, its weight, the elastic forces that it is under, and its distance from points of support. This time is called the natural period, and is the length of time required to complete one to-and-fro movement.
Natural tetrachord—A tetrachord built with the following intervals between its notes—a minor second, followed by a minor second, followed by a major second.
Natural triad—The major chord.
Neapolitan major scale—(*See Table X.*)
Neapolitan sixth chord—The triad on the lowered supertonic, in c minor, D flat-F-A flat, traditionally used in first inversion.

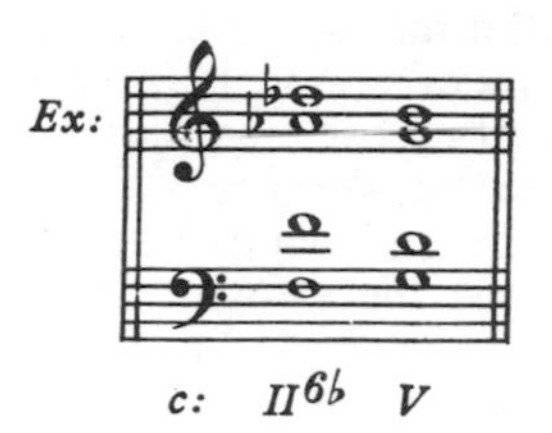

Neapolitan minor scale—(*See Table X.*)
Nearly related tonality—Tonality whose key signature differs by no more than one accidental.
Neck—That part of instruments of the violin and guitar family, which lies between the peg box and the belly.
Negligente (*It.*)—In a careless manner.
Neighboring tone—The upper or lower second of a harmonic tone which returns to the original tone. (*See Table XI.*)
Neue Musik (*Ger.*)—New music.
Neue Sachlichkeit (*Ger.*)—New objectivity. Used to designate the " no-nonsense " attitude which opposed the intense subjectivity of the expressionists.
Neume—A nod or a sign—signs or accents used to indicate the rise and fall of the voice.
Neumes—The factors of Middle Age notation.
Neutral syllable—A syllable such as " la " that is substituted for words, syllables, letters or numbers when reading music.
Nicht (*Ger.*)—Not.
Ninth—The interval of an octave and a second.
Ninth chord—A chord which consists of the third, fifth, seventh and ninth above the root.

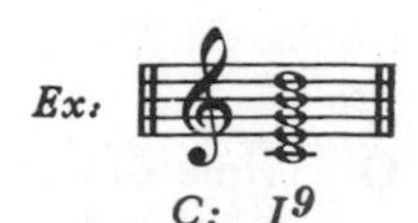

Nobile (*It.*), **Nobilmente**—In a refined, lofty style.
Nocturne (*Fr.*)—A piece of a romantic character.

Nodal figures (acoustics)—Points of perfect or comparative rest—figures corresponding to the " nodal lines " of a vibrating body.

Node (acoustics)—On a vibrating string, the point of least displacement.

Noel (*Fr.*)—A Christmas song; derived from nouvelles, meaning " tidings."

Noise (acoustics)—A sound with partials of irregular proportion (e.g., 1, 2/5, 3/7, etc.).

Noise music—The attempt to increase the material of music by including noises in order to reflect the complexity of modern life. Accomplished through the utilization of six families of noises to be reproduced mechanically, i.e. (1) booms, thunderclaps, explosions, etc.; (2) whistles, hisses, etc.; (3) whispers, murmurs, etc.; (4) screams, screeches, etc.; (5) noises obtained by percussion on metals, wood, etc.; and (6) voices of animals and men, shouts, shrieks, groans, etc.

Nomenclature—In music the terms applied to the various signs employed to stand as representatives of time, sounds, pitch, pace and expression.

Non (*It.*)—Not.

Nonad—Nine-note chord.

Non-essential tones—Tones which are similar to non-harmonic tones but which are not members of the accompanying harmony.

Nonet—A piece for nine performers.

Non-harmonic dissonance—A general term covering all tones which are dissonant and have their own characteristics of preparation and resolution.

Non-harmonic tones—Any tones which do not belong to the underlying harmony. (*See Table XI.*)

Non-metrical melody—A melody which does not contain a constant grouping of the tones into measures of equal duration.

Non-modulatory cadences—Same as modulatory cadences with all accidentals eliminated.

Nonuple meter (simple or compound)—Any meter that has nine beats to each measure.

Nonuplet—A group of nine notes of equal time value played in the time ordinarily allotted to six or eight of the same kind belonging to the regular rhythm.

Nota cambiata (*It.*)—A 16th century melodic device whereby a dissonance is left by a downward leap. (*See Table XI.*)

Notation—The science of expressing music in writing.

Note—A symbol used to express the pitch and duration of musical tones.

Notturno (*It.*)—Originally a serenade; now a piece of music of a quiet character.

Novelette—A name invented by Schumann and given by him to a set of pieces.

Nuance—Musical modification of intensity, tempo, touch, or phrasing.

Numerals—Numbers used instead of the names of notes, usually within a certain key having eight notes in the diatonic scale.

Nut—The ridge over which the strings pass at the end of the fingerboard next to the head of a violin or guitar, or other stringed instrument.

— O —

O—Triple or perfect time in medieval music. Placed over a note in stringed music it indicates an open string or harmonic. Also (*It.*) or, as, either.

Obbligato (*It.*)—A passage of such importance that it is obligatory, and cannot be omitted; sometimes a solo passage.

Oblique motion (*See Motion*)—One voice remaining on the same pitch while the other moves up or down.
Oboe (*It.*)—Oboe.
Octad—Eight-note chord.
Octave—An interval consisting of eight diatonic tones. The eighth tone of the diatonic scale. (*See Table VIII.*)
Octave-marks, 8va and 8va basso—When 8va is put over a note, the note is to be played an octave higher. A line extending from the 8va shows that all notes under the line are to be played an octave higher. 8va basso, placed under a note or notes, transposes an octave downward.
Octet—A composition for eight performers.
Octuple meter (simple or compound)—Any meter that has eight beats to a measure.
Octuplet—A group of eight equal notes having the same time value as six notes of the same kind in the regular rhythm.
Odeon (*Gr.*)—A building in which musical performances are given.
Oeuvre (*Fr.*)—Work; opus.
Off—In organ music, a direction to push in a stop.
Offen (*Ger.*)—Open.
Offertory—A hymn, prayer, anthem or instrumental piece sung or played during the celebration of Holy Communion or performed during the offering.
Ohne (*Ger.*)—Without.
Ohne Dämpfer (*Ger.*)—Without mute.
Ongarese (*It.*)—Hungarian.
Open diapason—An organ stop.
Open Harmony (*See Open structure.*)
Open notes—Of stringed instruments, the notes of the open strings. Of wind instruments the series of natural harmonies which can be produced by the lip without the assistance of a slide, key or piston.
Open strings—Strings producing the sounds assigned to them according to the system of tuning belonging to that particular instrument. Strings are " stopped " when their pitch is altered by the pressure of the finger.
Open structure—A spacing of the notes in a chord where there is more than an octave between the soprano and tenor.
Open vocal scores—A score in which each voice has its own individual staff.
Opera—The musical form of drama, set to music for voices and instruments and produced with scenic effects.
Operetta—A little opera.
Opposite motion—Same as contrary motion.
Opus (*Lat.*)—Work; used by composers to number the order in which their works are written.
Oratorio (*It.*)—A composition consisting of solos and concerted pieces for voices, the theme of which is taken from the Bible or from sacred history.
Orchestra—A group of musicians who perform on a collection of instruments in which strings are prominent, thereby distinguishing it from the band or wind ensemble.
Orchestration—The science of combining the instruments utilized in the symphony orchestra. The art of scoring music for an orchestra.
Order—Open and close order is synonomous with open and close structure.
Organ—A keyboard musical wind instrument containing various wooden or metallic pipes made to sound by means of compressed air from bellows, and played upon by means of keys.
Organ point—(*See Pedal point.*)

Organ tone—The tone of the eight-foot Open Diapason on the Great Organ manual. An organ-like tone produced by an instrumental or choral group.
Organum (*Lat.*)—Church music of the early Christian era characterized by two parts moving in parallel fourths and fifths.
Oriental scale—(*See Table X.*)
Original minor scale—Same as natural or pure minor scale.
Ornamentation—(1) A spontaneous act on the part of the interpreter who, in performing a written or traditional melody, enlivens it, expands it, or varies it through his technique of improvization; (2) a compositional technique; (3) the use of ornaments (trills, turns, etc.) in a melody. (*See Table XII.*)
Oscillograph (acoustics)—A machine which can produce a permanent picture of a sound wave.
Ossia (*It.*)—Or.
Ossicles (acoustics)—The middle ear contains a chain of three small bones, called the hammer, anvil and stirrup, and collectively called the ossicles.
Ostinato (*It.*)—Obstinate, continual, unceasing; a repeated motive or figure.
Ottava (*It.*)—Octave, 8va.
Ou (*Fr.*)—Or.
Ouvert (*Fr.*)—Open.
Overblowing (acoustics)—The phenomenon which occurs when a wind instrument is blown harder or with a different lip and tongue setting resulting in the harmonic particals becoming so prominent as to dominate the fundamental.
Overlapping phrases—The second phrase beginning simultaneously with the arrival of the last chord of the first phrase.
Overlapping voices—Two voices moving in similar motion, the lower voice moving higher than the pitch just left by the upper voice, or vice-versa.
Overtones (acoustics)—The tones generated above a fundamental tone by secondary vibrations of the main wave. (*See Table II.*)
Overtone scale—(*See Table X.*)
Overtone series—(*See Table II.*)
Overture—(1) An introductory symphony for instruments; (2) a prelude to an opera or oratorio.

— P —

P—Abbreviation for piano, meaning soft. Abbreviation for pedal.
Paired notes—Two parallel series of notes played on a keyboard instrument with one hand.
Pandiatonicism—A principle of formation, in which tonality reigns in the vertical sense but no corresponding tonal idea directs the horizontal succession.
Pan-rhythm—True transformation of traditional rhythmic ideas.
Pan's pipes—The earliest form of a wind instrument. It was formed of hollow-reeds of different lengths stopped at the bottom and blown into by the mouth at the top.
Pantomime—An entertainment in which not a word is spoken or sung, but the sentiments are expressed by gesticulation accompanied by music.
Pantonality—All-tonal in the strict sense of the word as opposed to tonality or atonality.
Parallel chords—The successive sounding of a fixed chordal combination, consonant, or dissonant, through various degrees of the scale.

Parallel fifths—Two voices moving in parallel motion from one perfect fifth to another perfect fifth.
Parallel intervals—The simultaneous progression of two parts in the same direction having the same intervallic relationship.
Parallel keys—The major and minor founded on same key note.
Parallel minor—A minor key having the same tonic note as a certain major key. Ex.: *c* minor, *C* major.
Parallel motion—Two or more melodic lines which move at the same interval spacing from one position to the next.
Parallel relationship—Two chords having two tones in common, the fundamental and the fifth.
Paraphrase—The adaptation of vocal or instrumental pieces for other media—an orchestration, bandstration, or choral arrangement.
Parlando (*It.*)—In a speaking or declamatory style.
Parlato (*It.*)—Spoken.
Partial (acoustics)—An overtone or harmonic generated by a fundamental tone. (*See Table II.*)
Partita (*It.*)—A suite.
Partitur (*Ger.*)—A full score.
Part-music—Harmonized music.
Part-singing—Performance of part-music.
Part-song—A composition for at least three voices in harmony, without accompaniment.
Part-writing—The technique of supplying the missing voices to any given voice or voices.
Pas (*Fr.*)—Not.
Passacaglia (*It.*)—Italian dance in triple meter written on a ground bass. A continuous variation based on a clearly distinguishable ostinato.
Passage—A term which is loosely used to refer to a short section of a composition.
Passing chords—Unessential chords which are the result of simultaneous passing tones.
Passing modulation—A temporary shift of tonality, usually occuring in a modulating sequence, moving immediately to another tonal center.
Passing note—A melodic note not essential to the harmony. (*See Table XI.*)
Passing tone (*See Non-harmonic*)—A non-harmonic tone which conjunctly connects two harmonic tones, usually a third apart. (*See Table XI.*)
Passione, con (*It.*)—Passionately.
Passion Music—Music set to the narrative of our Lord's Passion in the Gospel.
Pasticcio (*It.*)—A musical medley.
Pastoral—A scenic cantata—an instrumental piece depicting rural scenes.
Patetico (*It.*)—Pathetic.
Pauken (*Ger.*)—Timpani.
Pause—Also known as hold or fermata. Indicates that note or rest over which it appears is to be prolonged. (*See Table XIII.*)
Pavan—A stately dance in 4/4 meter of a stately character.
Pavillons en l'air (*Fr.*)—Bells in the air.
Pedal—Any mechanism controlled by the foot.
Pedal point—A sustained pedal or bass note, over which occur varying chords and harmonies. In modern usage, any tone or tones prolonged throughout changes in harmony.
Pelog scale—(*See Table X.*)
Pentad—Five-note chord.

Pentatonic—A scale of five tones. Also used to describe the most common pentatonic order as revealed by the intervallic relationship of the black keys of the keyboard. (*See Table X.*)
Percussion—Instruments that are struck, as a drum, bell, cymbals, etc.
Per (*It.*)—For, by, from, in, through.
Percussive harmony—Compound chords are often large and complex and when used in succession are effective as declamations, arrival points, and opening and closing statements. They form naturally percussive chords when the smaller intervals are low in the structure.
Perdendosi (*It.*)—Decreasing in power, dying away.
Perfect authentic cadence—A special cadence in which both the dominant and tonic chords have their roots in the bass and the soprano ascends or descends stepwise to the root of the tonic.
Perfect cadence—An arrangement of the V-I cadence in which the dominant and tonic chords are in root position and the tonic note in the soprano.
Perfect fifth—An interval comprised of seven semitones. (*See Table VIII.*)
Perfect fourth—An interval comprised of five semitones. (*See Table VIII.*)
Perfect intervals—The intervals of the octave with twelve semitones, the fifth with seven semitones, the fourth with five semitones, and the prime or unison. (*See Table VIII.*)
Perfect octave—An interval comprised of twelve semitones. (*See Table VIII.*)
Perfect plagal cadence—A plagal cadence in which the soprano note remains unchanged in the progression IV-I.
Perfect unison—An interval in which both notes are located on the same pitch. (*See Table VIII.*)
Period—A natural grouping of two phrases; a complete musical statement ending on a full close.
Pesante (*It.*)—Heavy, ponderous.
Petit (*Fr.*)—Little, small.
Petite Flute (*Fr.*)—Piccolo.
Petto (*It.*)—The chest.
Peu (*Fr.*)—Little, a little.
Pf.—Abbr. of (1) Pianoforte; (2) Pianoforte, soft then loud; Piu forte, louder.
Phase (acoustics)—The position of a particle of a vibrating body at any moment as a wave is being generated.
Phonograph—An instrument by means of which sounds can be recorded and reproduced.
Phrase—A natural division of the melodic line comparable to a clause of speech; it must have a cadence. Complete in one sense, it is incomplete in another.
Phrase-mark—A curved line connecting the notes of a phrase.
Phrase modulation—A modulation effected when the establishment of the new key is accomplished by means of the cadence which ends the phrase.
Phrases, irregular—Phrases containing more or less than the usual four or eight complete measures.
Phrasing—A system used in music to punctuate melodies much as a sentence is punctuated.
Phrygian cadence—A harmonic close which originated in the Phrygian mode as the final cadence. In modern usage, any transposition of the progression IV^6-V♯.
Phrygian mode—Similar to the natural minor scale, however, its second degree is lowered one-half step. (*See Table X.*)
Phrygian scale—(*See Table X.*)

Piacere (*It.*)—Pleasure. A piacere, at pleasure, as desired.
Piacevole (*It.*)—Pleasing, graceful.
Piangendo (*It.*)—Plaintively, sorrowfully.
Pianissimo (*It.*)—Very soft. Abbreviated to pp.
Piano (*It.*)—Soft. The name " piano," as applied to the instrument, comes from *Gravicembalo con piano e forte*, meaning a keyed instrument with both soft and loud tones.
Pianoforte (*It.*)—A keyboard stringed instrument—the tones being produced by hammers striking the strings. First developed by Bartolommeo Cristofori in 1711.
Piano staff—The " g " clef and the " f " clef with the middle C line omitted.
Piatti (*It.*)—Cymbals.
Picardy third—The practice of ending a composition in the minor mode on a major chord by chromatically raising the third of the final chord in the perfect cadence.
Piccolo (*It.*)—(1) Small; little; (2) a small flute.
Piece—A musical composition. Sometimes used in reference to an instrument or to a member of an instrumental group.
Piena (*It.*)—Full.
Pitch (acoustics)—The word used to indicate the relative highness or lowness of a tone. It is scientifically determined by the number of vibrations per second.
Pitch balance—The balance about some general level of pitch which a melodic line ordinarily possesses.
Pitch-pipe—A small reed-pipe which sounds tones of fixed pitch.
Piu (*It.*)—More.
Piu mosso, Piu moto (*It.*)—More motion, quicker.
Pivotal modulation—A modulation which involves a chord common to both keys.
Pivot chord—The chord used in a modulation which is common to both keys.
Pizzicato (*It.*)—The plucking of a string on a string instrument.
Placido (*It.*)—Placid, tranquil, calm.
Plagal cadence—The cadence progression from subdominant to tonic.
Plain chant—The plainsong.
Plainsong—(*See Gregorian Chant.*)
Plaque (*Fr.*)—Struck at once.
Plates (acoustics)—Plates are similar to rods in that they do not require stretching, as do membranes and strings. In this respect they may be thought of as " two-dimensional rods." Their edges are usually in vibration instead of being nodal lines as in stretched membranes.
Plectrum (*Lat.*)—A quill, or piece of ivory used to pluck the strings.
Plus (*Fr.*)—More.
Pochetto (*It.*)—A little.
Poco (*It.*)—Little, a little.
Poco a poco (*It.*)—Little by little.
Podatus—A kind of neume.
Poi (*It.*)—Then, after that, next.
Point d'orgue (*Fr.*)—Pedal point.
Pointe (*Fr.*)—At the point of the bow.
Pointillism—The fragmenting of melodic lines by dividing them between two or more voices.
Polacca—A Polish dance in 3/4 meter.
Polka—A dance in 2/4 meter, originated among the peasants of Bohemia.
Polka Mazurka—A mazurka danced with the polka step.

Polonaise (*Fr.*)—A Polish dance in 3/4 time and moderate tempo.
Polychords—Chord members are best arranged in resonant intervallic relationship; but if the arrangement produces two separate triadic units a polychord results.
Polymeter—When the pulse is irregularly but consistently subdivided, different time signatures are used simultaneously.
Polymodal—Involves two or more different modes on the same or different tonal centers. The modal strands may be melodic or harmonic.
Polymorphous counterpoint—Counterpoint which includes great variation of the theme.
Polyphonic—Music which is conceived as a combination of two or more melodies rather than a succession of chords accompanying one melody.
Polyphony—Music for several voices in which the melodic lines prevail over the harmonic element. Music that is composed of parts, or voices, which support one another, in contrast with homophony, which is melody supported by chords.
Polyrhythm—The simultaneous use of striking contrasting rhythms in different parts of the musical fabric, also known as cross rhythm.
Polytonality—The simultaneous presence of several different tonal centers.
Pomposo (*It.*)—Pompous.
Ponderoso (*It.*)—Ponderous; strongly marked.
Ponticello (*It.*)—An indication for the performer to bow the string near the bridge of a string instrument.
Portamento (*It.*)—A type of ornamental resolution of a suspension. The carrying over of one note into the next, so rapidly that the intermediate notes are not defined. In piano music, two or more notes under a slur, with dots above them; the notes to be played with some emphasis and separated slightly.
Portando (*It.*)—Carrying.
Portato (*It.*)—A dot with a short curved line over or under notes indicating a non-legato tone, but not as short as staccato.
Posato (*It.*)—Sedate, quietly.
Posaune (*Ger.*)—Trombone.
Position—(*See Open and Close Structure.*)
Position of the fifth—Occurs when the fifth of a chord is in the soprano.
Position of the octave—Occurs when the fundamental of a chord is in the soprano.
Position of the third—Occurs when the third of a chord is in the soprano.
Postlude—A closing voluntary on the organ.
Pot-pourri (*Fr.*)—A musical medley.
Pousse (*Fr.*)—Up bow. (*See Table XIII.*)
Pp—Abbr. of pianissimo.
Praeludium (*Ger.*)—(*See Mordant.*)
Precentor—The Master of the choir.
Precipitato (*It.*)—In a precipitate manner; hurriedly.
Precisione (*It.*)—Precision, exactness.
Prélude—A musical introduction to a composition or drama.
Preludo (*It.*)—Prelude.
Première (*Fr.*)—First.
Preparation—(1) The consonance immediately preceeding a dissonance; the treatment of dissonance controlled by its approach; (2) the up-beat preceeding the initial down-beat of a measure which indicates the tempo.
Près de la table (*Fr.*)—Near the harp sounding board.
Pressando (*It.*)—Pressing on; hurrying the time.

Prestissimo (*It.*)—Extremely fast; as fast as possible. The quickest tempo in music.
Presto (*It.*)—Very rapidly; quicker than any tempo except prestissimo.
Prima donna—The leading soprano; the soloist.
Prima vista (*It.*)—At first sight.
Prima volta—First time.
Primary accent—The thesis or down-beat. The first beat of the measure.
Primary harmonic functions—Tonic, subdominant and dominant.
Primary triad—One of the three fundamental triads of a key; includes all triads located on tonal degrees; I, IV and V.
Prime (unison)—Two tones of the same pitch. (*See Table VIII.*)
Primo (*It.*)—Principal, first.
Principal chord—(*See Primary triad.*)
Principal tones—Those tones referred to as the first, third and the fifth of the tonic triad.
Principal triads—Triads which establish a sense of tonality.
Principle of proximity—In the connection of two chords, the tonal movement of any one voice (soprano, alto or tenor) should usually produce the minimum amount of movement; that is, the second note (note of resolution) should be in close intervallic proximity to the first—seldom more than a third.
Probe (*Ger.*)—A rehearsal.
Programmed music—The generation of music by means of automatic high-speed digital computers.
Progress—The motion of one note to another note or one chord to another chord.
Pronunziato (*It.*)—Pronounced.
Proportion (acoustics)—An interval related to another interval in terms of frequencies of sound waves.
Prova (*It.*)—A rehearsal.
Psalm—A sacred song or hymn.
Psaltery—One of the most important of the stringed instruments of the ancient Hebrews.
Pulse—The underlying beat over which rhythm is superimposed. (*See Meter.*)
Punta d'arco (*It.*)—At the point of the bow.
Pure minor scale—The natural or pure minor scale differs from the major scale in that the third, sixth and the seventh degrees are lowered one-half step, both ascending and descending. (*See Table X.*)
Puzzle canon—(*See Enigma canon.*)
Pyramidal chords—A type of compound chord which is composed of a series of intervals diminishing from the bottom upward.
Pythagorean intonation (acoustics)—Used in the middle ages, it had the same arrangement of whole and half-steps that our modern major scale has; however, the ratios of whole and half-steps (hemitones) were different.

— Q —

Quadrat (*Ger.*)—The sign for a natural.
Quadratnotation—Square notation.
Quadrille (*Fr.*)—A French dance; consisting of five movements.
Quadruple counterpoint—Counterpoint of four parts so constructed that all the parts may be transposed among themselves without transgressing the laws of progression.

Quadruple meter—Regular grouping of the time units by four.
Quadruplet—Group of four equal notes executed in the time of three or six of the same kind in the regular rhythm.
Quality—The color of a tone. The difference between tones of the same pitch played on various instruments.
Quart—Interval of a fourth.
Quarter-note—A unit of music notation that receives one pulsation when the lower unit of the meter signature is four. It receives one-fourth the value of a whole note. (*See Table III.*)
Quarter rest—A rest equal in time value to a quarter note. (*See Table III.*)
Quartet—A composition for four performers.
Quartulet—Same as duolet with exception of four used instead of two.
Quasi (*It.*)—Almost, nearly.
Quasi-authentic cadence—A cadence in which each chord retains the quality it would normally have in the major mode.
Quartal harmony—Chords by fourths.
Quatre mains (*Fr.*)—For four hands.
Quatuor (*Fr.*)—Quartet.
Quaver—An eighth note. (*See Table III.*)
Queue (*Fr.*)—(1) Tail piece of a stringed instrument; (2) tail of a note.
Quickstep—A march in 6/8 meter.
Quindecima—The interval of a fifteenth—two octaves, 15ma. Alla quindecima indicates two octaves higher or lower.
Quint—Interval of a fifth.
Quinte, Quintsaite (*Ger.*)—The E string of a violin.
Quintet—A composition for five performers.
Quintole (*Ger.*), **Quintuplet**—A group of five notes to be played in the time of four of the same value. (*See Table VI.*)
Quintuple meter (simple or compound)—Any meter which has five beats to a measure.
Quintuplet—A group of five notes played in place of four.
Quire (*Old Eng.*)—The title of a body of trained singers in a church.
Quodlibet—(1) A sort of Fantasia; (2) a Dutch concert.

— R —

R (*Ger.*)—Abbreviation in English or German for right.
Rallentando (*It.*)--Making the tempo gradually slower.
Range—The number of notes a particular voice may sing or an instrument may play usually thought of in terms of highest note possible to lowest possible. (*See Tables XVI, XVII and XVIII.*)
Rapidamente (*It.*)—Rapidly.
Rarefaction (acoustics)—Occurs when the particles are farther apart than normally.
Rasch (*Ger.*)—Fast.
Rattenuto (*It.*)—Holding back.
Re (*It.*)—The syllable used in singing, etc., for the second note of the scale. The supertonic.
Reading—Performing a piece without rehearsal or specific preparation.
Real intervals—Two tones with a definite chord feeling.
Re bémol (*Fr.*)—The note D flat.
Recessional—The hymn sung at close of service.

Recht (*Ger.*)—Right, right-hand.
Recitativo (*It.*)—Declamatory singing.
Re dièse (*Fr.*)—The note D sharp.
Redoubled interval—Compound interval.
Redowa—A Bohemian dance.
Reduction—A small version of the original, such as reduced scores. The re-arrangement of a composition for a smaller number of instruments.
Reed—A thin strip of cane, wood or metal which, when set in vibration by a current of air, produces a musical sound.
Reel—A lively rustic dance.
Reflected sound waves (acoustics)—Sound waves coming in contact with matter whose density is greater than that of the medium through which they are traveling.
Reflection (acoustics)—The bouncing back of sound waves when they strike a surface, such as the walls, floor, or ceiling of a concert hall.
Reflective harmony—Any chord (Tertian, quartal, secundal, polychordal or compound) which is mirrored by adding below the original formation strictly inverted intervals in symmetrical reflection.
Reflective keyboard writing—That which produces unique mirror harmony that equalizes the movement of the hands and creates simultaneous and uniform keyboard technique. Simultaneous inversion beginning at any of the pivotal points produces strict mirroring regardless of what type of harmony is used; the fingering in both hands will, without exception, be identical.
Refraction (acoustics)—The bending of a wave front, due to a change in the density of the material through which it is passing, or to a wind effect.
Refrain—The chorus at the end of every stanza of some songs.
Register—(1) On the organ, the set of pipes controlled by a single stop; (2) the whole compass or one of the sections of the voice.
Registration—The combination of stops in organ playing.
Rehearsal, Probe (*Ger.*), **Prova** (*It.*)—A general practice before a performance.
Related—A term applied to those chords or keys which allow for an easy and natural transition from one to the other.
Relationship—Degree of affinity between keys, chords and tones.
Relative chord—A common chord made up of notes taken from the scale.
Relative key—Refers to a key which has the same key signature as its major or minor counterpart.
Relative major—A major key is relative to that minor key, the tonic of which lies a minor third below its own.
Relative minor—A minor key is relative to that major key, the tonic of which lies a minor third above its own.
Relative pitch (acoustics)—The pitch of a tone in relation to a standard tone or a given key.
Religioso (*It.*)—Religiously; solemnly.
Remote key—An unrelated key. (*See Foreign tonalities.*)
Renvoi (*Fr.*)—A repeat.
Repeat—A sign signifying that the music between [repeat sign] and [repeat sign] is to be repeated. (*See Table XIII.*)
Repercussion—Repetition of a tone or chord.
Repetition—To repeat an entire piece of music or any part thereof.
Replicato (*It.*)—Repeated.
Repos (*Fr.*)—A pause.

Repose chord—The tonic chord as opposed to the dominant chord which is an active chord.
Reprise (*Fr.*)—(1) Chorus of a song; (2) a repeat.
Requiem (*Lat.*)—Rest. The first word in the Mass for the dead.
Resin—Rosin.
Resolution—The tendency of chords to progress toward a point of rest. The strict treatment of dissonance regarding the leaving of the dissonant interval.
Resolution, irregular—A departure from the customary practice of voice leading or resolution for a purely harmonic matter of root progression.
Resolution, ornamental—An interpolation of one or more tones between a dissonance and its resolution. (*See Table XI.*)
Resonance (acoustics)—The transmission of vibrations from one vibrating body to another.
Response—The answer to a versicle in the church service.
Rest—A symbol used to indicate relative periods of silence. (*See Table III.*)
Retardation—A suspension which resolves upwards.
Retarded progression—(*See Retardation.*)
Retrograde—Moving backwards.
Retrograde canon—(*See Canon Crancrizan.*)
Retrograde inversion—The combination of retrograde motion and inversion.
Retrograde motion—Occurs when a melodic line is written backwards.
Retrogression—Chords moving in opposite direction from the normal progression. (*Ex.: Normal progression, IV-V; Retrogression, V-IV.*)
Reveil, Revelly (*Old Eng.*)—Music which wakens from sleep. Signal given to soldiers at dawn.
Reverberation (acoustics)—The phenomenon of a continuing roll of sound.
Reverberation time (acoustics)—The length of time that a sound continues to be heard in a room, through reflections, after its source has stopped sounding.
Reverse motion—Contrary motion.
Reversion—Retrograde imitation.
Rf—Abbreviation of Rinforzando.
Rhapsodie or Rhapsody—Brilliant composition of irregular form.
Rhythm—The principle of alternating tension and relaxation in the duration of tones. The interference of sounds against an underlying pulse.
Rhythm, harmonic—The pattern of the distribution of chord changes in a phrase; the relationship of meter to harmonic progression.
Rhythmic dictation—Development of the ability to reproduce, in notation, the rhythms heard.
Rhythmic reading—Reproducing at sight only the durations represented by the symbols in printed music.
Rhythmic repetition—The durational values of a group or figure remaining the same, but with varied pitches.
Ribattuta (*It.*)—A beat.
Ricercare (*It.*)—16th and 17th century vocal or instrumental composition, developed in rather complex contrapuntal style from several motives.
Riddle canon—(*See Enigma canon*).
Rigaudon (*Fr.*)—A lively French dance.
Rigore (*It.*)—Exactness of tempo.
Rigoroso (*It.*)—In strict time.
Rinforzando (*It.*)—Reinforced, accented.
Ripetizione (*It.*)—Repetition.
Risoluto (*It.*)—Resolute, hold.

Rit.—Abb. of Ritardando.
Ritardando (*It.*)—Retarding, delaying the time gradually.
Ritardation—A suspension which resolves upward.
Ritenuto (*It.*)—Retained, kept back; more slowly.
Ritournelle (*Fr.*), **Ritornello** (*It.*)—A short prelude, interlude or postlude to an air. Italian folk song.
Rods (acoustics)—One-dimensional, like strings, rods are inherently elastic, needing no stretching. Their ends are usually " loops " instead of nodes.
Romance—A ballad in the Romance dialect—short instrumental pieces romantically cast.
Roman numerals—Figures used to identify chords. (*Ex.: I, II, III, IV, V, VI, VII.*)
Romantique (*Fr.*)—In the style of a romance.
Rondeau (*Fr.*)—A form of music frequent in monophonic songs of the 13th century.
Rondo (*It.*)—An instrumental piece characterized by the principal theme being repeated after each new theme is introduced.
Root—The generating note of a triad or any of its inversions or modifications.
Rootless harmony—Chords by perfect fourths are ambiguous in that, like all chords built by equidistant intervals, any member can function as the root.

Root position chord—Occurs when the root of the triad is placed in the bass or lowest voice.

Root transformation—Occurs when a chord has been altered to such an extent that the root becomes ambiguous.
Rosalia (*It.*)—The repetition of a phrase or passage, raising the pitch one note at each repetition.
Rosin—A gum, the exudation of certain trees, which, when properly prepared, is used to rub over the hair of a bow.
Roulade (*Fr.*)—A florid vocal phrase.
Round—A vocal canon for two or more voices or instrumental lines at the unison or octave.
Roundel—A dance in which all joined hands in a ring.
Rubato (*It.*)—A style of playing in which one note may be extended at the expense of another, for purposes of expression.
Ruhig (*Ger.*)—Quiet, calm.
Ruhrtrommel (*Ger.*)—Tenor drum.
Rullante (*It.*)—Rolling.
Rumba—A Cuban dance with emphasis primarily on rhythm.
Run—A rapid succession of notes.
Rustico (*It.*)—Rural, rustic.

— S —

S.—Abbreviation for " segno," sign; " senza," without; " sinistra," left; " subito," suddenly.
Sackbut—Bass trumpet, with slide like a trombone.

Sacred music—Music written primarily for the church service.
Saite (*Ger.*)—String.
Saltarello (*It.*)—An Italian dance.
Salto (*It.*)—A leap or skip.
Sanctus (*Lat.*)—A part of the Communion service in the Church of England, and a part of the Mass in the Church of Rome.
Sanft (*Ger.*)—Soft, mild.
Sans (*Fr.*)—Without.
Sans sourdine (*Fr.*)—Without mute.
Saraband—A dance of Spanish origin utilizing two eight measure reprises in slow tempo in triple meter.
Sarrusophone—A brass wind-instrument with a double reed.
Saxhorn—A brass wind-instrument with three, four or five cylinders.
Saxophone—A metal wind-instrument with single reed and clarinet-like mouthpiece.
Scale—A series of tones, comprised within an octave. (*See Chromatic*, *Major*, *Minor*, *etc.*) The arrangement according to increasing or decreasing pitch within one octave of the tonal material of a mode, or system, or composition. (*See Table X.*)
Scale, tempered—A scale made up of intervals that deviate from the pure, acoustically correct intervals.
Scandicus flexus (*Lat.*)—A kind of neume.
Schalltrichter auf (*Ger.*)—Bells in the air.
Schellentrommel (*Ger.*)—Tambourine.
Scherzando (*It.*)—Jestingly.
Scherzo (*It.*)—A jest, or play. A piece in lively tempo and jesting style.
Schlag (*Ger.*)—A stroke or beat.
Schleifer (*Ger.*)—Slurred note.
Schleppend (*Ger.*)—Dragging, drawling.
Schluss (*Ger.*)—The conclusion.
Schlüssel (*Ger.*)—A clef.
Schmerz (*Ger.*)—Grief.
Schmetternd (*Ger.*)—Brassy.
Schnell (*Ger.*)—Quick, rapid.
School—(1) A method or system of teaching; (2) a group of composers whose works mark an epoch in the history of music.
Schottische—A round dance, similar to the polka, in 2/4 meter.
Schwermuthig (*Ger.*)—Sad, pensive.
Sciolto (*It.*)—Light, free.
Scordato (*It.*)—Out of tune.
Scordatura (*It.*)—A special tuning for string instruments.
Score—A manner of writing music which shows all the parts of an ensemble arranged vertically.
Score, piano—An arrangement for the piano of choral or instrumental music.
Scoring—Instrumentation, orchestration. The art of notating for instrumental or choral groups.
Scorrendo (*It.*)—Glissando, gliding from one tone to another.
Scotch snap—A sixteenth note followed by a dotted eighth note.
Se (*It.*)—If.
Sec (*Fr.*)—Dry, plain.
Secco (*It.*)—Unornamented.
Second—The interval between two conjunct scale degrees. (*See Table VIII.*)
Second classification—Chords which have their roots on the subdominant

or supertonic and progress normally to chords of the first classification.

Second inversion chord—Occurs when the fifth of a triad is placed in the bass or lowest voice.

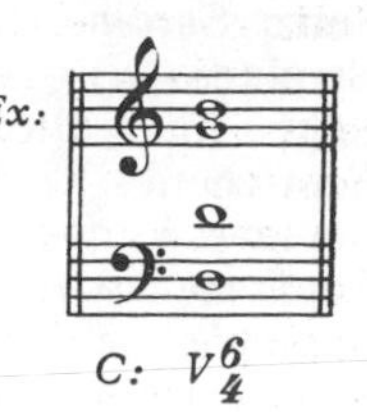

Secondary chords—Subordinate chords.
Secondary dominant—The dominant chord of a chord on any degree of a scale. (*See Tonicization.*)
Secondary seventh chords—A term including all diatonic seventh chords except the V^7.
Secondary triads—The supertonic, mediant, submediant, and subtonic chords of any major or minor key.
Second ending—The symbols, 1 2 in combination with a repetition sign, means that the first ending is to be played before the repetition, the second ending after.

Second inversion seventh chord—Occurs when the fifth of the seventh chord is placed in the bass/or lowest voice.

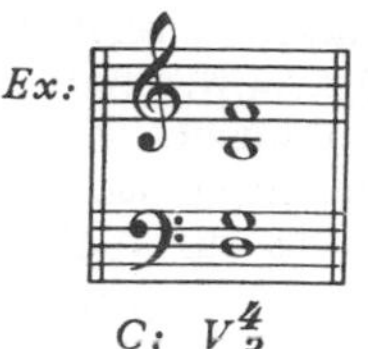

Secondo (*It.*)—Second part.
Section—The unit next larger than a bar. A section may be two or three bars or half a phrase.
Sectional fugue—A fugue whose form is not adaptable to two-part nor three-part categories.
Secular music—Music other than that for the church.
Secundal harmony—Chords by seconds or sevenths.
Segno (*It.*)—A sign. (*See Table XIII.*)
Segue (*It.*)—It follows; now follows. Used to denote: (1) a continuance of a certain style (*See Simile*), or (2) a linking of movements or pieces with no pause.
Seguidilla (*Sp.*)—Vivacious Spanish dance in 3/4 or 3/8 meter.
Sehr (*Ger.*)—Very.
Semibreve—A whole note. (*See Table III.*)
Semi-cadence—(*See Half Cadence.*)
Semidemiquaver—A thirty-second note. (*See Table III.*)
Semiquaver—A sixteenth note. (*See Table III.*)
Semitone—The half of a whole tone; the smallest interval of European music.
Semplice (*It.*)—Simple, in a pure style.
Sempre (*It.*)—Always; constantly.
Sensible (*Fr.*)—Leading note of a scale; major seventh.
Sensible (*It.*)—Expressive.
Sentence—Synonymous with period. (*See Period.*)
Sentie (*Fr.*)—Expressed.

Senza (*It.*)—Without.
Senza Sordino (*It.*)—Without mute.
Se piace (*It.*)—At will.
Sept—Interval of a seventh.
Sept-chord—Seventh chord.
Septet—A musical group containing seven players.
Septième (*Fr.*)—The interval of a seventh.
Septuple meter (compound or simple)—Any meter having seven beats to a measure.
Septulet—A group of seven equal notes to be played in the time of four or six of the same kind in the regular rhythm.
Sequence—A systematic transposition of a motive to different scale degrees. May be literal (modulating) or diatonic (non-modulating).
Serenade—An instrumental or choral composition short or rather simple in character.
Serenata (*It.*)—An 18th century dramatic cantata. An instrumental composition having five or more movements, similar to the suite and the symphony, but freer in form.
Sereno (*It.*)—Serene; tranquil.
Serial harmony—When harmony is regulated by a horizontal, unifying idea (twelve-tone or not), the texture may be serial; this kind of writing creates harmony of extraordinary compactness through the manifold variations of the motif relationships.
Serial music—Term used interchangeably with twelve-tone music and dodecaphonic music. Music based on a series of notes chosen from the twelve tones of the chromatic scale. Such a series, or row as it is called, functions in some ways as a scale does in tonal music in that it serves as the raw material out of which the composition is made.
Serioso (*It.*)—Gravely, seriously.
Service—A term in church music signifying a musical setting of those portions of the offices sung by a choir.
Sestet—A sextet.
Sestetto (*It.*)—A sextet.
Sestole, Sestolet (*It.*)—A sextuplet.
Settimino (*It.*)—A septet.
Seventeenth—A tierce. An interval of two octaves and a third.
Seventh—The interval located seven diatonic steps away from the prime. (*See Table VIII.*)
Seventh chord—A seventh chord is a four-tone chord built in thirds above a given root. Its name is derived from the interval formed between the root, third and chord seventh when the chord is in root position.

Sext—Interval of a sixth.
Sextet—A musical group containing six players.
Sextole, Sextolet—A sextuplet.
Sextuple meter (simple or compound)—Any meter having six beats to a measure.
Sextuplet—A group of six equal notes to be performed in the time of four of the same kind in the regular rhythm.
Sf or Sfz—Abbreviation for " Sforzando " or " Sforzato."
Sforzando (*It.*)—Forced, accented. Abbreviated of Sf.
Shading—The combination and alternation of any or all of the varying degrees of tone power between FFF and ppp.

Shake—A trill.
Sharp—The notation (♯) placed before the head of a note raises its pitch one-half tone.
Sharp (adjective)—Too high in pitch.
Shift—In string playing, a change of position.
Si (*It.*)—The syllable used to denote the seventh note of the scale.
Si bémol (*Fr.*)—The note B flat.
Siciliano (*It.*)—A moderately slow dance of pastorale character in 6/8 or 12/8 meter.
Sight singing—Reading and singing a piece of music without rehearsal or specific preparation.
Sign—A note or character employed in music. (*See Table XIII.*)
Signature, key—A grouping of frequently used accidentals in a composition. (*See Table IX.*)
Signature, meter—Number placed at the beginning of a composition indicating the type of meter and the unit of beat.
Silenzio (*It.*)—Silence. A pause.
Silofono (*It.*)—Xylophone.
Similar motion—Two parts moving in the same direction, but not necessarily the same distance.
Simile (*It.*)—Similarly.
Simple—Not compound or complex.
Simple beat—A beat which has a background of two equal pulsations.
Simple meter (*See Simple beat.*) (*See Table IV.*)
Sin' al fine (*It.*)—To the end.
Sine curve (acoustics)—The curve, regular and symmetrical, reflected on a graph of simple harmonic motion.
Sinfonia (*It.*)—A symphony or opera-overture.
Sinfonietta (*It.*)—A small symphony.
Single meter (simple or compound)—Any meter having one beat to a measure.
Singstimme (*Ger.*)—A vocal part.
Sinistra (*It.*)—Left hand.
Sino, Sin (*It.*)—To, toward, as far as.
Sinusoidal sounds—Pure sounds divested of their overtones.
Sixteenth note (Semiquaver)—A unit of music notation that receives one-half the time value of an eighth note. (*See Table III.*)
Sixth—The interval located six diatonic steps away from the prime. (*See Table VIII.*)
Skip—A melodic interval of more than a second.
Skizzen (*Ger.*)—Sketches; short pieces.
Slargando (*It.*), **Slentando** (*It.*)—Becoming gradually slower.
Slide—A movable tube in the trombone. Also to pass from one note to another without any cessation of sound.
Slur—A curved line drawn over two or more notes to indicate that they are to be played legato.
Smorzando (*It.*)—Dying away.
Soavemente (*It.*)—Sweetly, delicately.
Soggetto (*It.*)—Subject, theme.
Sognando (*It.*)—Dreaming; dreamily.
Sol (*It.*)—The syllable denoting the fifth note of the scale.
Sol-bémol (*Fr.*)—Note G flat.
Solennita (*It.*) **con.**—With solemnity.
Sol-fa—Refers to the singing of solfeggi to the solmization-syllables.

Sol-faing—A system of singing. A composition in which the names of the notes are employed instead of the words.
Solfège (*Fr.*)—Syllables of solmization of the scale such as: do, re, mi fa, sol, la, ti (si), do.
Solfeggio (*It.*)—Vocal exercise on the solmization syllables.
Solmization—Guido d'Arezzo's method of teaching scales and intervals by syllables.
Solo (*It.*), **Soli (plural)**—Alone.
Somma (*It.*)—Utmost.
Son (*Fr.*)—Sound, tone.
Sonare (*It.*)—To sound, to play upon.
Sonata (*It.*)—An instrumental composition, usually for a solo instrument, in three or four contrasting, extended movements.
Sonata-Allegro form—A ternary form usually applied in the first movement of a sonata. It usually deals with two or three themes set in the form of (1) exposition, (2) development, and (3) recapitulation. (*See Table XV.*)
Sonatina (*It.*)—A short sonata. Usually in two or three movements, sometimes written as one long movement.
Sonatina form—(*See Table XV.*)
Song—A short poem with musical setting.
Song form—A vocal or instrumental composition comprised of two, three or more sections.
Sonore (*Fr.*), **Sonoro** (*It.*)—Sonorous, resonant.
Sopra (*It.*)—Above, over before.
Soprano (*It.*)—The highest voice in a four-part composition.
Soprano clef—(*See Table VII.*)
Soprano range (voice)—(*See Table XVI.*)
Sordamente (*It.*)—Softly, gently.
Sordino (*It.*)—Mute. A small contrivance to dampen or deaden the sound of an instrument.
Sospirando (*It.*)—Sighing; very subdued.
Sospiro (*It.*)—A crotchet or quarter rest. (*See Table III.*)
Sostenuto (*It.*)—Sustaining the notes to their full length.
Sotto (*It.*)—Under, below.
Sotto voce (*It.*)—Softly, with subdued voice.
Sound (acoustics)—Vibration produced by a vibrating body, transmitted through a medium by means of sound waves and picked up by a receiving device such as the human ear.
Sound-board—The general term for the piece of fir or other resonant wood used in the construction of various instruments.
Sound post—A small post, or prop, within a stringed instrument.
Sound wave (acoustics)—The continuation of a sound vibration through an adjacent medium such as air.
Soupir (*Fr.*)—A crotchet or quarter rest. (*See Table III.*)
Sourdine (*Fr.*)—Muted.
Sous (*Fr.*)—Under.
Space—The interval between two lines in the staff.
Spacing—The vertical arrangement of the notes of a chord.
Spelling—The selection of notes to form intervals and/or chords usually upward on the staff. The actual naming of the notes in a logical manner to form intervals or chords.
Spianato (*It.*)—Smooth, even; legato.
Spiccato (*It.*)—Separated, detached; a semi-staccato for violin, obtained

by brushing the strings lightly with the bow and lifting it off quickly.

Spinet—An ancient keyed instrument similar to a small harpsichord. The smallest of the modern pianos.

Spiral canon—A canon in which the melody ends in a different key from the one in which it began.

Spirito (*It.*)—Spirit; fire; energy.

Spitze (*Ger.*)—At the point of the bow.

Springing bow—A style of bowing in which the bow is allowed to bounce on the strings.

Stabat Mater—A Latin hymn on the Crucifixion, sung during Passion Week in the Roman Catholic Church.

Stabile (*It.*)—Steady, firm.

Staccato (*It.*)—Detached; separate. A manner of performance indicated by a dot placed over the note, calling for a reduction of its written duration with a rest substituted for half or more of its value.

Staff—A series of horizontal equal distant lines, now invariably five in number, upon which the musical notes are written.

Standard Pitch—In May, 1939, at the International Conference on Pitch, held at London, $a^1 = 440$ vibrations per second was unanimously adopted as the standard pitch.

Stark (*Ger.*)—Strong; vigorous.

Static harmony—An absence of root change in a harmonic progression.

Stationary waves (acoustics)—Two waves of equal length and equal amplitude, traveling in opposite directions at the same rate of speed, and passing over each other.

Stem—A vertical line attached to a note head.

Stentando (*It.*)—Delaying; retarding.

Stentato (*It.*)—Forced; emphasized.

Step—The interval between two contiguous degrees of a scale.

Steso (*It.*)—Extended.

Stesso (*It.*)—The same.

Stop—To press the finger on the string of a stringed instrument. (Noun) a rank, or set or organ pipes.

Strain—A period, sentence, or short division of a composition; a motive or theme.

Strascino (*It.*)—A drag or slur.

Strathspey—A Scottish dance in duple meter.

Strepito, con (*It.*), **Strepitoso** (*It.*)—In a noisy, boisterous, impetuous style.

Stretta (*It.*)—A coda in swift tempo.

Stretto (*It.*)—Literally, pressing on or forward, referring to the overlapping of the subject in two or more voices. Like inversion, it may occur in any pitch relationship.

Strict counterpoint—An academic discipline employed in teaching beginning counterpoint, based on the melodic and harmonic materials of pre-17th century vocal composition.

Strict style—A composition written in traditional style with regularly prepared and resolved dissonances.

String—Prepared wire, silk, catgut or plastic, plain or covered, used for musical instruments.

Stringendo (*It.*)—Hurrying, accelerating the tempo.

Stringere (*It.*)—To hasten.

String Gauge—A contrivance for measuring the thickness of strings.

String Quartet—A composition in four parts for two violins, viola and 'cello.

Strophic form—Form in which the same music is repeated for each verse.
Structure—The result of vertical placement of notes in a chord. (*See Open structure; Close structure.*)
Study—A composition in the style of an exercise to facilitate the acquirement of some special difficulty.
Style—A distinctive or characteristic mode of presentation, construction or execution in the art of music.
Styrienne (*Fr.*)—An air in slow movement and 2/4 meter, often in minor.
Sub (*Lat.*)—Under; below; beneath.
Sub-contra octave—(*See Table I.*)
Subdivision of the background—Division of the beat (simple or compound) into two, three or four equal durations.
Subdominant (Fa) (*See Degree*)—Referring to the fourth degree of the scale.
Subdominant cadence (Plagal) (*See Cadence*)—The cadence progression from subdominant to tonic.
Subito (*It.*)—Suddenly, immediately.
Subject—Theme. A melodic motive or phrase on which a composition is founded.
Submediant (La) (*See Degree*)—Referring to the sixth degree of the scale.
Suboctave—The octave below a given tone.
Subordinate chords—Chords built on the second, third, sixth and seventh scale degrees—all seventh chords except the dominant seventh.
Subordinant triads—Triads erected on scale tones other than the tonic, dominant and subdominant.
Subsonics (acoustics)—Vibrations of the air having frequencies below approximately twenty per second.
Substitute functions—A term applied to cases in which a chord normally identified with one degree is used where the clear harmonic effect is that of another.
Substitution—In contrapuntal progression, the resolution or preparation of a dissonance by substituting, for the regular tone of resolution or preparation, its higher or lower octave in some other part.
Subtonic—The scale degree located one whole tone below the tonic.
Suite (*Fr.*)—A series or set of movements in various dance forms.
Suivez (*Fr.*)—Follow.
Sul (*It.*)—Upon, near.
Sul ponticello (*It.*) (*Ger.*)—Near the bridge.
Sul tasto (*It.*)—On the fingerboard.
Summation tones (acoustics)—Tones which have frequencies equal to the sum of the frequencies of the two tones which generate them.
Super (*Lat.*)—Above; over.
Superdominant—The sixth degree of a diatonic scale. (*See Submediant.*)
Superimposed backgrounds—Durations based upon compound divisions introduced into simple meter or vice versa. (*See Table VI.*)
Superimposed meter—Durations based upon triple meter introduced into duple meter or vice versa. (*See Table VI.*)
Superior relative triad—Higher in pitch than one it is related to.
Super Locrian scale—(*See Table X.*)
Superoctave—The octave above a given tone.
Supersonics (acoustics)—Vibrations of the air having frequencies above approximately 20,000 per second.
Supertonic (Re) (*See Degree*)—Referring to the second degree of the scale. (*See Table X.*)
Sur (*Fr.*)—Upon; on; over.

Sur la chevalet (*Fr.*)—Near the bridge.
Sur la touche (*Fr.*)—On the fingerboard.
Suspension—Highly important as a means of emotional expression—particularly in its relationship to the principle of tension and release. The tension, generated by the dissonant suspended tone, is dissipated when the dissonance resolves to the note of resolution. The three elements of the suspension pattern are commonly referred to as the preparation, suspension and resolution. A melodic device delaying the entrance of an expected tone; also, the delaying (or suspended) tone itself. (*See Table XI.*)
Sussurando (*It.*)—Murmuring.
Sustain—To perform in sostenuto or legato style; to sustain during the full time value.
Sustained Note—A name given to prolonged notes which partake of the character of a pedal point.
Svegliato (*It.*)—Brisk; lively.
Swell—Crescendo (<), as opposed to diminuendo (>). (*See Table XIII.*) Also, the name applied to one of the manuals on the Organ: Swell Organ.
Syllabic declamation—The use of one note for each syllable of text.
Symmetrical scale—(*See Table X.*)
Sympathetic vibration (acoustics)—One body of material is capable of absorbing energy of the other which is in motion, if the two bodies have the same period of vibration.
Symphony—An orchestral composition usually containing the following movements or movements of similar relationhips: I. Allegro; II. Adagio; III. Scherzo; IV. Allegro.
Syncopate—To efface or shift the accent from a strong beat to a weak beat
Syncopation—The deliberate upsetting of the normal pulse of meter, accent and rhythm.
Synthetic music—Electronic music.
System—Where two or more portions of a score appear on one page, each such portion (suggested either by a space or two short parallel lines //) is called a system.

— T —

T—An abbreviation of Tasto, Tempo, Tenor, Toe (in organ music) and Tutti.
Tablature (*Fr.*)—(1) A general name for all the signs and characters used in music; (2) a peculiar system of notation used for instruments of the string class and certain wind instruments.
Tacet (*Lat.*)—Silence. Parts are marked tacet in instrumental or choral music which are not wanted for a movement or section.
Tail—Same as stem.
Takt (*Ger.*)—Beat, measure, time.
Tambour (*Fr.*)—Snare drum.
Tambour de Basque (*Fr.*)—Tambourine.
Tambourine—An instrument of the drum class, formed of a hoop of wood or metal, over which is stretched a piece of skin. The sides of the hoop are pierced with holes, into which are inserted metal jingles.
Tambour major (*Fr.*)—Drum major.
Tamburino (*It.*)—Tambourine.
Tamburo (*It.*)—Snare drum.

Tamburo Rullante (*It.*)—Tenor drum.
Tam-tam (*It.*), (*Fr.*), (*Ger.*)—Gong.
Tango—Popular Argentinian dance in duple meter.
Tanto (*It.*)—So much; as much; too much.
Tanz (*Ger.*)—A dance.
Tarantella (*It.*)—An Italian dance in 6/8 meter.
Tasto (*It.*)—Touch, key or keyboard of piano or organ.
Tasto Solo (*It.*)—Play. Melody in unison or octaves (without chords).
Tatto (*It.*)—The touch.
Te—Sometimes used for Si in tonic sol-fa.
Technicon—A mechanism for strengthening the fingers and increasing their flexibility.
Technique—The mechanical skill which is the foundation of the mastery of an instrument or type of composition.
Tedesco (*It.*)—German; in German style.
Temperament—The division of the scale into semitones. Those systems of tuning in which the intervals deviate from the acoustically correct intervals used in the Pythagorian system. (*See Equal temperament.*)
Tempestoso (*It.*)—Tempestuous.
Tempo (*It.*)—Time, with regard to speed; the pace at which a composition is to be performed.
Ten.—Abbreviation of " tenuto."
Tendency tones—Tones created by chromatic alteration. *Ex:*
Teneramente (*It.*)—Tenderly; delicately.
Tenerezza (*It.*)—Tenderness.
Tenor—In part music, the part above the lowest. The highest natural voice of men. (*See Table XVI.*)
Tenor clef—A symbol which locates c¹ (middle c) on the fourth line of the five-line staff; sometimes used in choral music for the tenor part, and by 'cello, trombone and bassoon. (*See Table VII.*)
Tenor range (voice)—(*See Table XVI.*)
Tension—Feeling generated by a dissonant suspended tone which is relieved when the dissonance resolves to the note of resolution.
Tenth (interval)—An interval comprised of an octave and a third.
Tenuto (*It.*)—Held, sustained for full value.
Tercet (*Fr.*)—A triplet.
Ternary form—Music which is divided into three parts.
Tertian harmony—Chords by thirds.
Terzetto (*It.*)—Usually a vocal trio; a composition for three performers.
Terzina (*It.*)—A triplet.
Tessitura (*It.*)—The location of a majority of tones in a piece or song.
Testo (*It.*)—Text; theme; subject.
Tetrachord—A succession of four tones which is the basis for constructing a scale. Two disjunct tetrachords make up one scale.
Tetrad—Four-note chord.
Tetralogy—A connected series of four music dramas.
Text—Words to which music is set.
Thematic composition—Contrapuntal treatment or development of one or more themes.
Theme—A subject. A musical motto which serves as the basis of a composition or movement.

Theory of Music—The science of music.
Thesis—The technical term meaning the " down-beat " of a phrase.
Third—The third degree of the diatonic scale and the interval thus formed. (*See Table VIII.*)
Third classification—Chords which have their roots on the submediant and progress normally to chords of the second classification.

Third inversion seventh chord (4/2)—A chord in which the seventh of the seventh chord is placed in the bass or lowest voice.

Ex: C: V_2^4

Thirty-second note—A note having three flags attached to its stem. (*See Table III.*)
Thorough-bass—A method of indicating an accompanying part by the bass notes together with figures designating the chief intervals and accompanying harmony. (*See Figured Bass.*)
Ti—A syllable sometimes used for the seventh note of the scale, in place of Si, which is too sibilant.
Tie—A curved line placed over a note and its repetition to show that the two shall be performed as one unbroken note. (*See Table XIII.*)
Tied notes—Notes which are joined together by a tie.
Third stave—A name given to the stave upon which pedal music is written for the organ.
Tief (*Ger.*)—Deep; low.
Tierce—A third.
Tierce de Picardie—(*See Picardy third.*)
Timbales (*Fr.*)—Timpani.
Timbre (*Fr.*)—Quality of tone; determined by the prominence of overtones.
Time—Customarily used for meter; i.e., the number of beats in a bar; as 3/4 time, 4/4 time, etc. It is more specific to use the word meter instead of time, to avoid confusion with tempo.
Time accent—The elongation of a second unit of a two-unit group of notes.
Time signature—(*See Meter Signature.*)
Timoroso (*It.*)—Timorous, hesitating.
Timpani (*It.*)—Timpani.
Tirade—The filling up of an interval between two notes with a run.
Tirato (*It.*)—(1) A down bow; (2) a scale passage in notes of equal length.
Toccata (*It.*)—Literally, a " touch piece "; now any keyboard piece.
Tonal center—The tone or harmony which determines the relative consonant and dissonant values of all other melodic and harmonic elements in a composition. The " key note " or tonic of a given key.
Tonal changes—Repeating motival tones, changing any tone or tones of the motive, or adding tones in a repetition of a motive.
Tonal degrees—The tonic, dominant and subdominant degrees.
Tonality—All notes in the scale related to one central tone; includes all harmony related to a given tonic chord. May include major and parallel minor keys. The totality of the melodic and harmonic elements of a musical work, as related to a common tonal center.
Tonal magnetism—The tendency of an active tone to resolve to a passive tone.
Tonal order—The pattern of keys on the keyboard (e.g., white keys—diatonic order).

Tonal sequence—A non-modulating sequence with one tonal center throughout.
Tonart (*Ger.*)—Scale; mode; key.
Tondichtung (*Ger.*)—Tone poem.
Tone—The building material of music. A tone possesses pitch, loudness, timbre and duration. It is produced by a regular vibration of an elastic body.
Tone clusters—Three or more adjacent tones sounding simultaneously.
Tone, common—A tone that is common to two successive chords in a progression.
Tone, non-chord—A tone in the melody which is not a part of the harmony written below it. (*See Table XI.*)
Tone row—An arbitrary arrangement of the twelve chromatic tones.
Tone, tendency—A desire for resolution of a tone created by dissonances and chromatic alterations which serve to augment the feeling of tonality inherent in the combination of leading-tone, dominant root and chord seventh.
Tonic Chord—The common chord of which the tonic is the root.
Tonic (Do) (*See Degrees*)—Referring to the first degree of a scale.
Tonicization—The process whereby harmonies other than the tonic are given greater vividness or emphasis.
Tonic sol-fa—Based on the movable Do system invented by Sarah Ann Glover in England about 1812. Do equals the tonic tone of any given key.
Tonic seventh chord—An active chord demanding resolution—usually down a fifth to IV or occasionally up a second to II.
Tonic triad—The triad which occurs on the tonic.
Tonkunst (*Ger.*)—Tone art; music.
Tonleiter (*Ger.*)—Scale.
Tonsatz (*Ger.*)—A composition.
Torsional vibration (acoustics)—Vibration in which the displacements are neither transverse nor longitudinal, but in a twisting direction.
Tosto (*It.*)—Quick.
Touch—The art of depressing the piano keys so as to produce a musical tone; also the resistance of the piano keyboard.
Touches (*Fr.*)—Keys of a pianoforte.
Toujours (*Fr.*)—Always.
Toye—A 16th and 17th century piece composed for the Virginal.
Tragicamente (*It.*)—Tragically.
Tranquillo (*It.*)—Tranquil, calm.
Transcription—An arrangement of a piece for some voice or instrument, or combination of, other than that for which it was originally intended.
Transferred resolution—On a chord repetition, the resolution of a dissonance in another voice.
Transient—Not principal; passing; intermediate.
Transition—Modulation; passing modulation.
Transpose—To write or perform a piece in a different key.
Transposing instruments—Instruments whose parts require a transposition from the true sounding pitches. (*See Table XVIII.*)
Transposition—The process of shifting music from one tonality to another.
Transverse waves (acoustics)—Waves which travel along a stretched string and are reflected at the ends to superpose on each other and produce standing waves.
Tre (*It.*)—Three.
Treble—The highest part of a choral composition. Soprano. The name usually associated with the " g " clef.

Treble staff—The staff with the " g " placed on the second line of a five-line staff.
Tremolo (*It.*)—A trembling or quavering; the rapid repetition of a note. On stringed instruments the quick reiteration of the same tone. In singing, a slight fluctuation of pitch. In keyboard music the rapid alternation of two or more pitches.
Tremoloso (*It.*)—With a tremulous, quavering effect.
Tremulant—An organ stop which produces primarily a variation of the loudness of the tone rather than of its pitch.
Très (*Fr.*)—Very.
Triad—Fundamental harmony consisting of root, third and fifth. (Major, Minor, Augmented, Diminished.) (*See Table XIV.*)
Triangel (*Ger.*)—Triangle.
Triangle—A steel rod bent into three-sided shape, struck with a small bar.
Triangolo (*It.*)—Triangle.
Trill—A musical ornament consisting of the rapid alternation of a given note with the diatonic second above it. (*See Table XII.*)
Trio (*It.*)—A piece for three parts or three voices. The division between the first theme and its repetition in marches and minuets.
Trionfale (*It.*)—Triumphal.
Trio sonata—Baroque chamber music with two upper voices and a thorough bass.
Triple counterpoint—In three-part contrapuntal writing, triple counterpoint occurs when the order of the three voices is completely invertible.
Triple meter—Regular grouping of time units by three.
Triplet—A group of three notes to be performed in the place of two of the same kind, indicated by a three and usually a bracket.
Tristezza (*It.*)—Sadness, pensiveness.
Tritone—The interval of three whole tones, the augmented fourth or diminished fifth, a strong dissonance. (*See Diabolus in Musica.*)
Trochaic—The name for the first of six rhythmic modes utilized in a 13th-century system of rhythm.
Tromba (*It.*)—A trumpet; also an eight-foot reed organ-stop.
Trombone—A metal wind-instrument of the trumpet family. It consists of two tubes, sliding in and out of the other.
Trompete (*Ger.*)—Trumpet.
Trompette (*Fr.*)—Trumpet.
Troppo (*It.*)—Too much.
Trumpet—A metal wind-instrument with cupped mouthpiece and small bell.
Tuba—The lowest pitched instrument in the brass family.
Tumultuoso (*It.*)—Vehement.
Tune—An air, melody. The act of adjusting the pitch of an instrument.
Tuning—The adjustment of an instrument to a recognized pitch.
Turca (*It.*)—In Turkish style.
Turn—An ornament consisting of a group of four or five notes which wind around the principal note. (*See Table XII.*)
Tutta (*It.*)—All; the whole.
Tutti (*It.*)—In orchestral works, the parts for the whole orchestra as distinct from that of the soloist.
Tutto (*It.*)—All; the whole.
Twelfth (interval)—An interval comprised of an octave and a fifth.
Twelve-tone technique—A system of composition in which the twelve chromatic tones are considered equally important and are related one to another.

Twenty-second (interval)—A triple octave.
Tympanic membrance (acoustics)—A thin membrane at the eardum about a three-hundredth of an inch thick.
Tyrolienne (*Fr.*)—A Tyrolese song for dancing.

— U —

U.C.—Abbreviation of " una corda."
Uebergang (*Ger.*)—Passage; transition.
Uebung (*Ger.*)—An exercise.
Uguale (*It.*)—Equal; like.
Umore (*It.*)—Humor; playfulness.
Un poco (*It.*)—A little.
Un, uno, una (*It.*)—One, a, an.
Una Corda (*It.*)—On one string only; in piano music it means to use the soft pedal.
Undecad—Eleven-note chord.
Undecuplet—A group of eleven equal notes to be played in the time of eight (or six) notes of like value in regular rhythm.
Undertone series—An intervallic reflection of the overtone series. (*See Table II.*)
Unequal voices—Mixed voices. Voices different in compass and quality.
Unessential tone—Tones in a musical fabric which do not coincide with the accompanying harmonic elements. (*See Non-harmonic tone.*) (*See Table XI.*)
Unis (*Fr.*)—In unison.
Unison (prime)—Two tones with the same letter name.
Unisono (*It.*)—Unison.
Uniti (*It.*)—After " divisi," the work Uniti is used to indicate that the performers again perform their parts in unison.
Unusual meter—Any meter that is not built on the traditional 1-2-3-4-5-6-7-8-9-12 beats per measure.

Ex.: $\frac{4\frac{1}{2}}{4}$

Up-beat—One or several initial notes of a melody which occur before the first bar line. (*See Anacrusis.*)
Ut (*Fr.*)—The syllable used by the French, in instrumental music, instead of Do, to designate the first note of the scale, or C.
Ut bémol (*Fr.*)—The note C flat.
Ut dièse (*Fr.*)—The note C sharp.
Ut supra (*Lat.*)—As above; as before.

— V —

V—An abbreviation for Verte, Violin, Volti, Vòce.
Va (*It.*)—Go on; continue.
Vacillante (*It.*)—To be performed in a wavering, hesitating style.
Value—Relative to the duration of a note or rest.
Valve—In brass wind instruments, a device by means of which brass tubes may be made to sound the semitones and tones between the natural open harmonics.
Valzer (*It.*)—Waltz.

Vamp—To improvise an accompaniment.
Variable Do—(*See Movable Do.*)
Variante (*It.*)—A variant; an optional reading.
Variation—A transformation of a theme by means of harmonic, rhythmic or melodic changes.
Varsovienne (*Fr.*)—A slow Polish dance in 3/4 meter.
Veloce (*It.*)—Swiftly.
Velocity of sound waves (acoustics)—Approximately 1,131 feet per second in air at 68 degrees Fahrenheit.
Ventil, Ventile—A valve.
Venusto (*It.*)—Beautiful; graceful.
Verschiebung (*Ger.*)—The soft pedal.
Verse—A stanza.
Versetzen (*Ger.*)—To transpose.
Verstimmt (*Ger.*)—Out of tune.
Verzierungen (*Ger.*)—Embellishments. (*See Table XII.*)
Vezzoso (*It.*)—Tender, sweet.
Via Sordino (*It.*)—Take off mute.
Vibrato (*It.*)—Recurrent swells and subsidences in a tone. On stringed instruments the slight fluctuation of pitch produced on sustained notes by an oscillating motion of the left hand. In singing, a scarcely noticeable wavering of tone.
Vibrating string (acoustics)—The instrument used to illustrate the nodes and antinodes making up a sound wave.
Vibration—(*See Cycle.*)
Vide (*Fr.*), **Vido** (*It.*)—Open.
Viel (*Ger.*)—Much.
Viertelnote (*Ger.*)—A quarter note. A crotchet note. (*See Table III.*)
Vif (*Fr.*)—Lively.
Vigoroso (*It.*)—Vigorous, bold.
Villanella (*It.*)—16th century Italian vocal music of a light-hearted nature.
Viol—An old instrument similar to the violin, but a little larger with six strings.
Viola (*It.*)—Viola.
Violin—The most important of modern solo and orchestral instruments. A gracefully shaped wooden box, with four strings, and played by means of a bow.
Violin clef—The G clef. (*See Table VII.*)
Violine (*Ger.*)—Violin.
Violino (*It.*)—Violin.
Violon (*Fr.*)—Violin.
Violoncell (*Ger.*)—Violoncello.
Violoncelle (*Fr.*)—Violoncello.
Violoncello (*It.*)—A four-stringed bow instrument shaped like a violin and held, while playing, between the knees.
Virginal—A stringed instrument played by means of a keyboard like the piano.
Virtuoso, -a (*It.*)—A great artist-performer, instrumentally or vocally.
Vite (*Fr.*)—Quickly.
Vivace (*It.*)—A brisk, animated tempo.
Vivacissimo (*It.*)—Very lively and fast.
Vivo (*It.*)—Lively; animated.
Vocal—Belonging to the voice; music intended to be sung.
Vocalion—A variety of reed organ.
Vocalize (*Fr.*)—A vocal exercise or etude.

Vocalization—The manner of singing.
Voce (*It.*)—The voice.
Voice—The sound produced by the human organs of speech; also, one of the parts in a composition.
Voice crossing—The writing of four-part music in which a certain voice is above or below an adjacent voice (e.g., alto above soprano or tenor below bass).
Voice leading—In polyphonic music, the principles governing the progression of the various voice parts—particularly of those other than the soprano.
Voicing—The arrangement of voices in a vertical harmonic structure.
Voix (*Fr.*)—The voice.
Volante (*It.*)—Flying; applied to the rapid execution of a series of notes.
Volata (*It.*)—A run.
Volkslied (*Ger.*)—A folk song.
Voll (*Ger.*)—Full.
Volonté (*Fr.*)—At will.
Volta (*It.*)—Turn; or time.
Volteggiando (*It.*)—Crossing the hands in pianoforte playing.
Volti (*It.*)—Turn.
Volume (acoustics)—The effect caused by the amplitude of the sound wave. The greater the displacement, the greater the volume or intensity, and vice versa.
Voluntary—An organ solo played before, during, or after any office of the church.
Vorhalt (*Ger.*)—A suspension.
Vorschlag (*Ger.*)—Appoggiatura; beat. (*See Table XII.*)
Vorspiel (*Ger.*)—A prelude.
Vortrag (*Ger.*)—Style of performance or interpretation.
Vorzeichnung (*Ger.*)—Signature. (*See Table IX.*)
Vox (*Lat.*)—Voice.
Vuidé (*Fr.*)—Open.

— W —

Waits, or Wayghtes—Originally minstrels attached to the households of kings or other prominent persons.
Waldhorn—A forest or hunting horn, also applied to the French horn.
Wallpaper music—Isolated phrases repeated over and over again, like the pattern of wallpaper. Sometimes referred to as " pedestrian " music.
Waltz—A round dance in triple meter.
Walzer (*Ger.*)—Waltz.
Wave (acoustics)—One complete cycle or vibration wave illustrated by the vibrating string.
Wave length (acoustics)—The distance traveled by a sound wave in one complete cycle.
Wave shape (acoustics)—Waves produced by each type of instrument giving it its quality.
Weber-Fechner law (acoustics)—States that equal increments of sensation are associated with equal ratios, or equal increments of the logarithm of the stimulus. In the case of loudness, the sensation of loudness-difference depends not on the difference in intensities involved, but on their ratio.
Wedge—Another name for the dot used to indicate some form of staccato. (*See Table XIII.*)

Weich (*Ger.*)—Minor; also soft; gentle.
Wenig (*Ger.*)—Little; a little.
White noise—All the sounds and all their overtones, even as white light includes the entire spectrum of color.
Whole note (Semibreve)—The second largest single unit of modern music notation, receiving a duration value of four pulsations in 4/4 meter. (*See Table III.*)
Whole rest—A pause equal in length to a whole note. (*See Table III.*)
Whole-step—The combination of two half-steps. (*See Half-step.*)
Wholetone—A major second.
Wholetone scale—A scale composed of only six tones, all distant a whole step from each other. (*See Table X.*)
Whori (acoustics)—Areas of higher air pressure created as streams of air pass over an edge.
Wind gradients (acoustics)—Differences in wind velocity caused by refraction.
Wind instruments—Musical instruments whose sounds are produced by the breath of the player, or by means of bellows.
Wirbel (*Ger.*)—Peg of a violin.
Wolf (1) The bad effect produced when playing in certain keys on an organ tuned to " unequal temperament "; (2) some note often found on an instrument, the intonation of which is not true.
Wood wind—The flutes, oboes, clarinets, bassoons, saxophones and similar instruments in a band or orchestra.

— X —

Xylophone—An ancient instrument, consisting of wooden bars, tuned to the tones of the scale and struck with mallets.

— Y —

Yang kin—A Chinese instrument with brass strings, which are struck with two small hammers.
Yo—An Indian flute.
Yodel or Jodel—The peculiar warbling of the Swiss or Tyrolean mountaineers.

— Z —

Zapateado (*Sp.*)—Spanish dance in triple meter.
Zart (*Ger.*)—Gently; tenderly; softly.
Zeichen (*Ger.*)—A musical character.
Zele (*Fr.*), **Zelo** (*It.*)—Zeal; energy.
Zeitmass (*Ger.*)—Tempo.
Ziemlich (*Ger.*)—Somewhat; rather.
Zierlich (*Ger.*)—Graceful; neat.
Ziffern (*Ger.*)—To cypher.
Zikrs—In Egypt the religious dances of the dervishes.
Zingareska—A gypsy song or dance.
Zinke (*Ger.*)—Cornet.
Zither (*Ger.*)—A flat stringed instrument.

Zögernd (*Ger.*)—Retarding, hesitating.
Zu (*Ger.*)—Too, to, by.
Zurückhalten (*Ger.*)—To hold back, to retard.
Zusammen (*Ger.*)—In unison.
Zwei (*Ger.*)—Two.
Zweihändig (*Ger.*)—For two hands.
Zweistimmig (*Ger.*)—For two voices.
Zwischenräume (*Ger.*)—Spaces of the staff.
Zwischensatz (*Ger.*)—An episode.
Zwischenspiel (*Ger.*)—An interlude.
Zymbel (*Ger.*)—Cymbal.

TABLE I

OCTAVE REGISTERS

Below "Middle C"

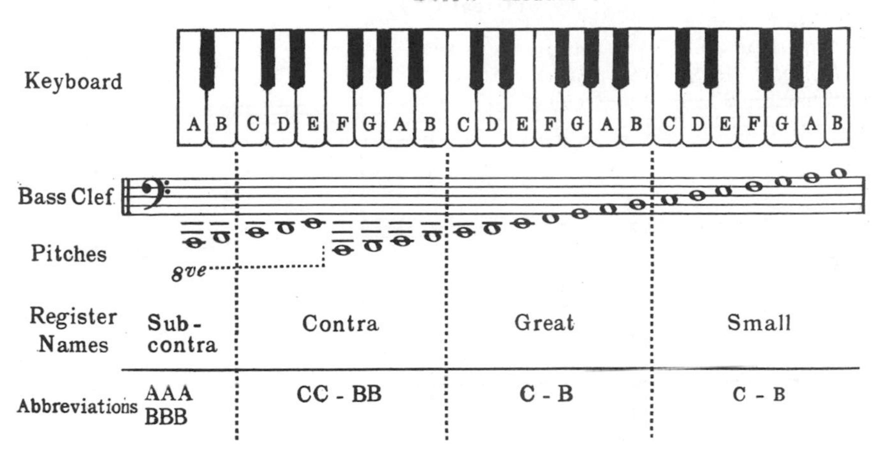

Above "Middle C"

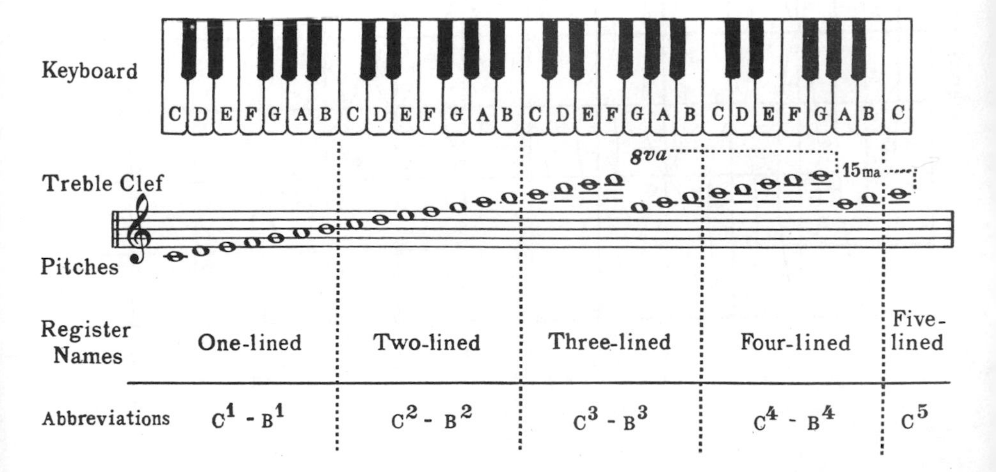

TABLE II

OVERTONE SERIES

Harmonics Generated by a Fundamental
(Great C*)

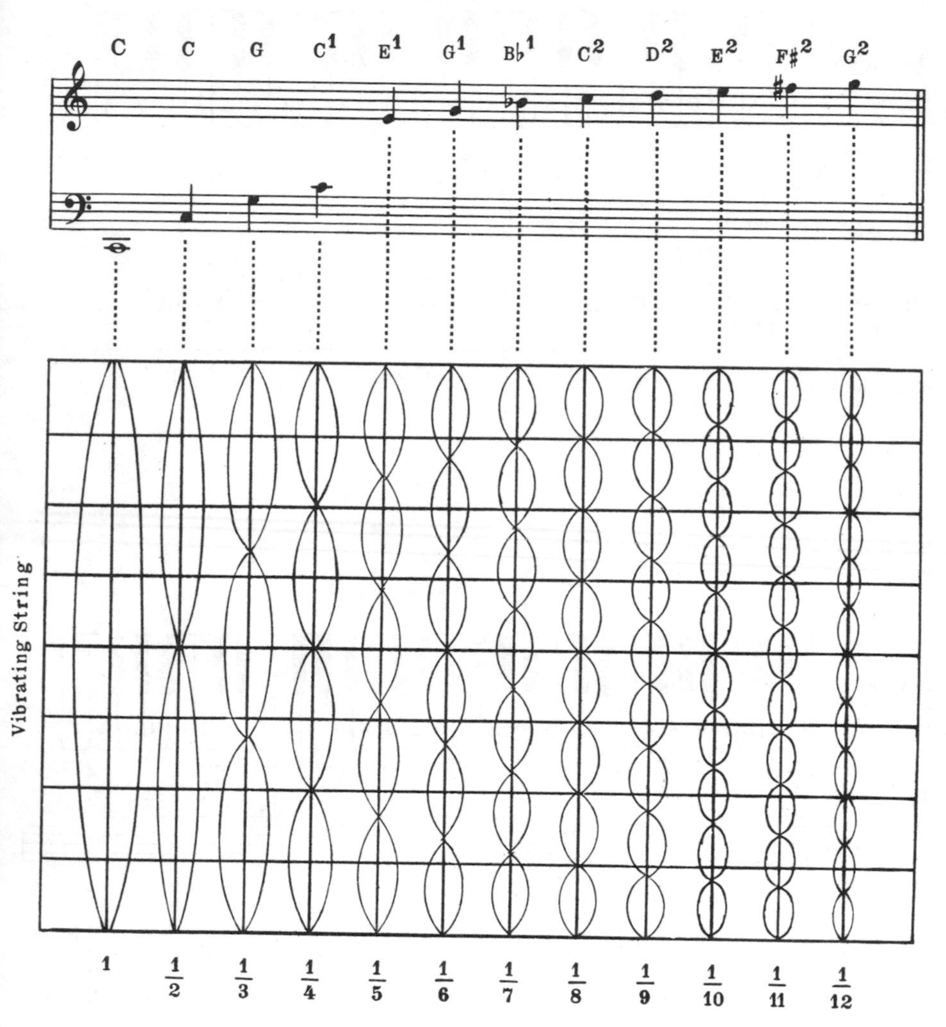

*Harmonics are generated by any given note serving as the fundamental producing the same intervallic relationship.

TABLE III

NOTATION

Simple			Compound		
NOTES		*RESTS*	*NOTES*		*RESTS*
𝅜	Double Whole (Breve)	𝄺	𝅜.	Dotted Double Whole (Dotted Breve)	𝄺.
𝅝	Whole (Semi-Breve)	𝄻	𝅝.	Dotted Whole	𝄻.
𝅗𝅥	Half (Minim)	𝄼	𝅗𝅥.	Dotted Half	𝄼.
𝅘𝅥	Quarter (Crotchet)	𝄽	𝅘𝅥.	Dotted Quarter	𝄽.
𝅘𝅥𝅮	Eight (Quaver)	𝄾	𝅘𝅥𝅮.	Dotted Eight	𝄾.
𝅘𝅥𝅯	Sixteenth (Semiquaver)	𝄿	𝅘𝅥𝅯.	Dotted Sixteenth	𝄿.
𝅘𝅥𝅰	Thirty-Second (Demisemi-quaver)	𝅀	𝅘𝅥𝅰.	Dotted Thirty-Second	𝅀.
𝅘𝅥𝅱	Sixty-Fourth (Hemidemi-semiquaver)	𝅁	𝅘𝅥𝅱.	Dotted Sixtyfourth	𝅁.

TABLE IV

METERS

SIMPLE METERS

DUPLE	*TRIPLE*	*QUADRUPLE*
$\frac{2}{2}$ = (2/ 𝅗𝅥)	$\frac{3}{2}$ = (3/ 𝅗𝅥)	$\frac{4}{2}$ = (4/ 𝅗𝅥)
$\frac{2}{4}$ = (2/ ♩)	$\frac{3}{4}$ = (3/ ♩)	$\frac{4}{4}$ = (4/ ♩)
$\frac{2}{8}$ = (2/ ♪)	$\frac{3}{8}$ = (3/ ♪)	$\frac{4}{8}$ = (4/ ♪)
$\frac{2}{16}$ = (2/ 𝅘𝅥𝅯)	$\frac{3}{16}$ = (3/ 𝅘𝅥𝅯)	$\frac{4}{16}$ = (4/ 𝅘𝅥𝅯)

COMPOUND METERS

DUPLE	*TRIPLE*	*QUADRUPLE*
$\frac{6}{4}$ = (2/ 𝅗𝅥.)	$\frac{9}{4}$ = (3/ 𝅗𝅥.)	$\frac{12}{4}$ = (4/ 𝅗𝅥.)
$\frac{6}{8}$ = (2/ ♩.)	$\frac{9}{8}$ = (3/ ♩.)	$\frac{12}{8}$ = (4/ ♩.)
$\frac{6}{16}$ = (2/ ♪.)	$\frac{9}{16}$ = (3/ ♪.)	$\frac{12}{16}$ = (4/ ♪.)

TABLE V

CONDUCTING FRAMES

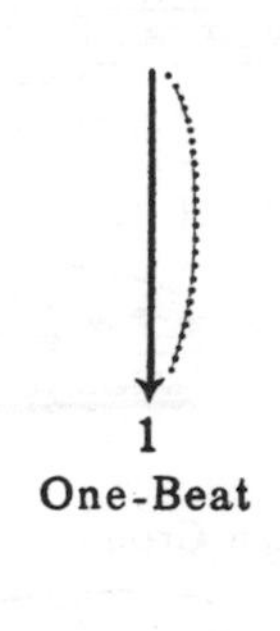

One-Beat

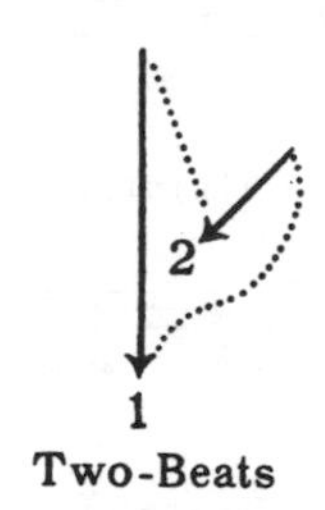

Two-Beats

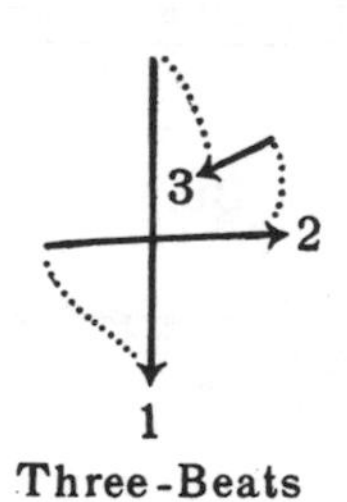

Three-Beats

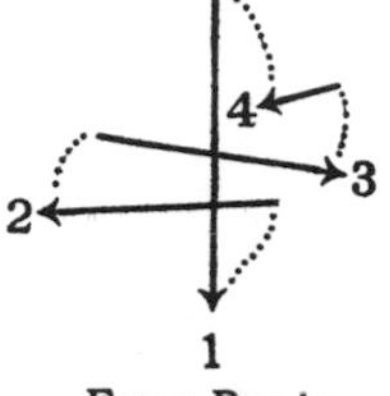

Four-Beats

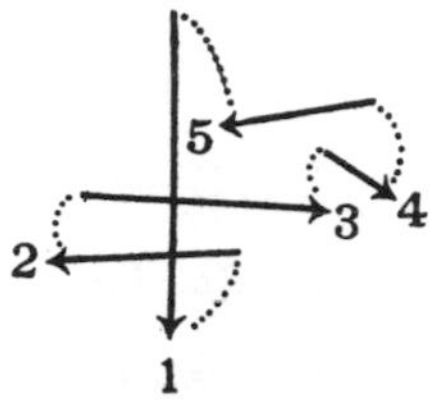

Five-Beats

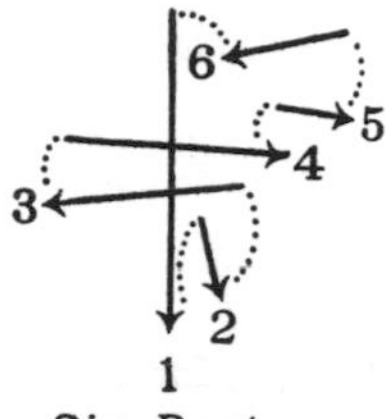

Six-Beats

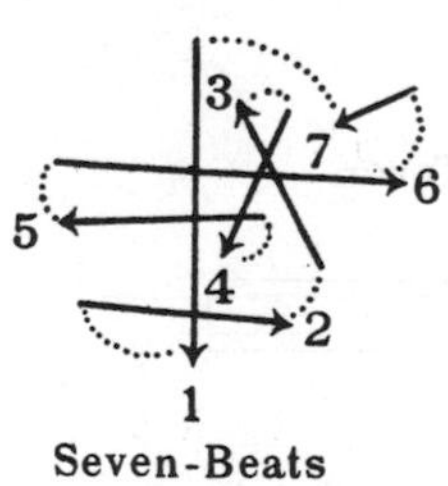

Seven-Beats

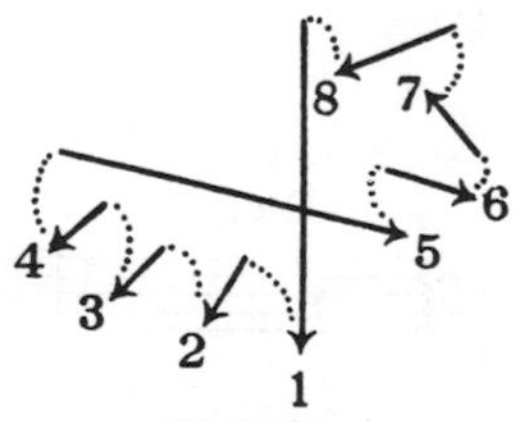

Eight-Beats

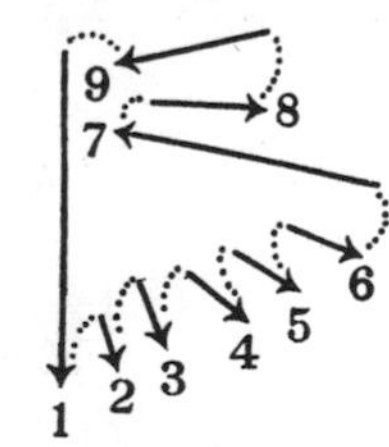

Nine-Beats

⟶ Indicates beat

.... Indicates preparation of beat

TABLE VI

ARTIFICIAL RHYTHMIC GROUPINGS

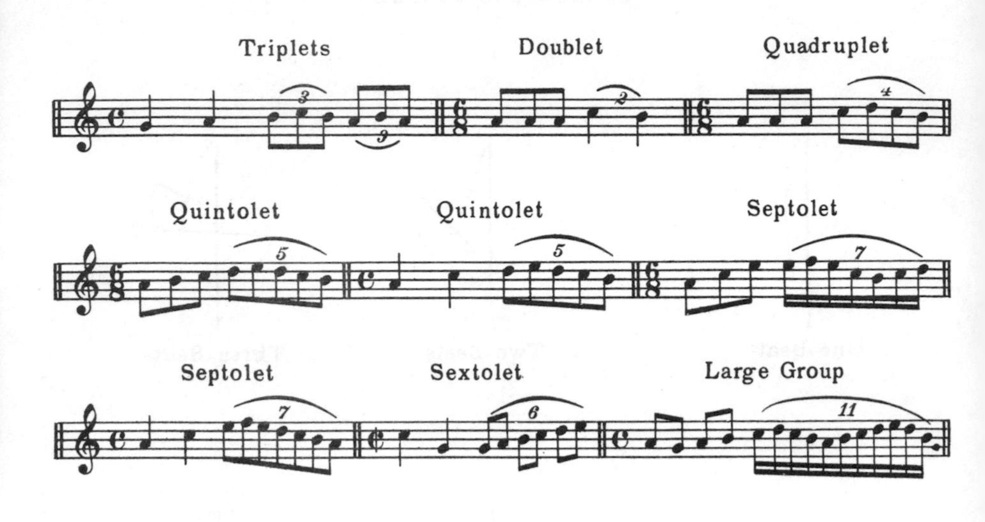

TABLE VII

CLEFS

Indicating the relative position of "Middle C"

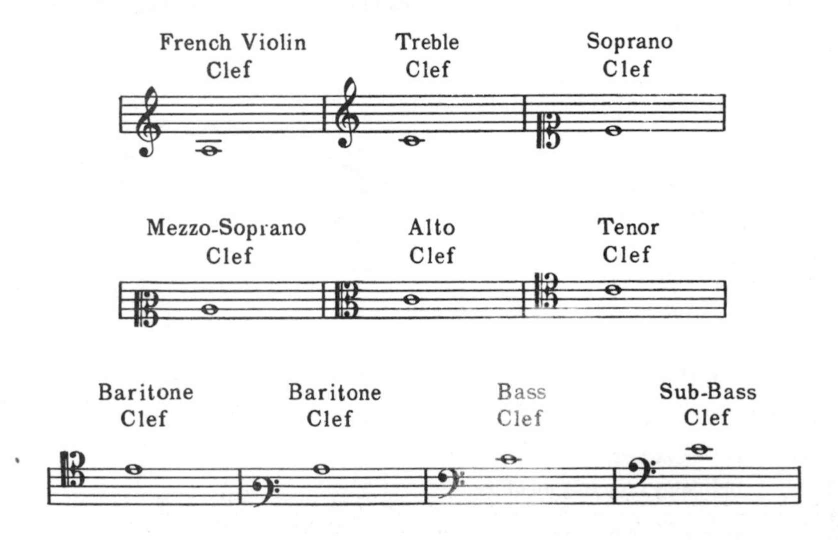

TABLE VIII

INTERVALS

NAMES	*ABBREVIATIONS*
Perfect	P
Prime	p
Major	M
Minor	m
Augmented	A
Diminished	d
Doubly Augmented	DA
Doubly Diminished	Dd

INVERSIONS

P(A)5 — P(d)4
m2 — M7
m3 — M6

Perfect 5th, when inverted, becomes Perfect 4th, etc.

EXPANSION AND CONTRACTION OF INTERVALS

Smaller ← → Larger

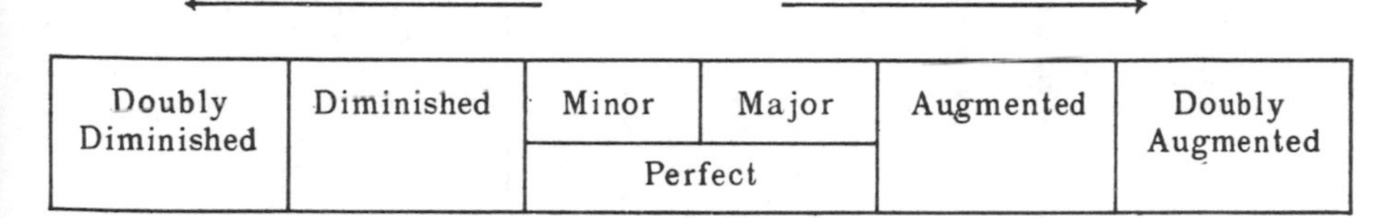

Doubly Diminished	Diminished	Minor	Major	Augmented	Doubly Augmented
		Perfect			

INTERVALS

Diatonic Interval Construction

EXAMPLES OF TYPES OF INTERVALS

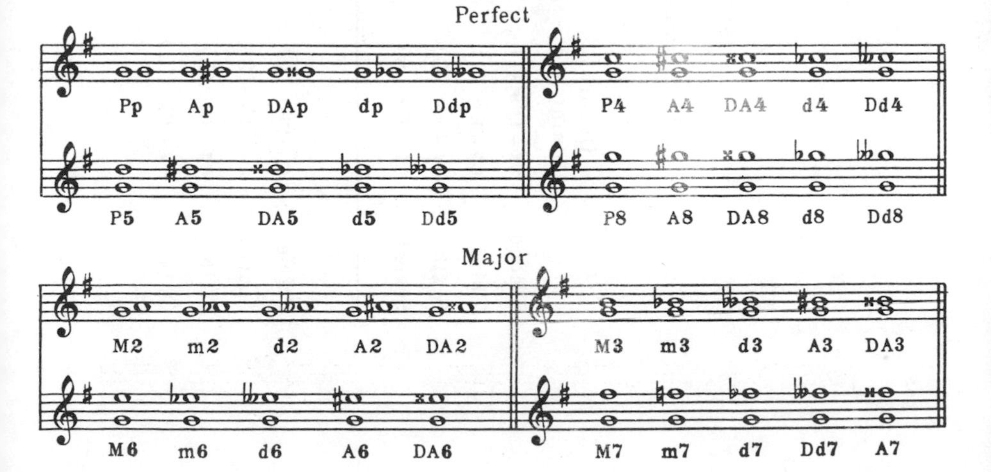

TABLE VIII (continued)

CLASSIFICATION AND TERMINOLOGY OF INTERVALS

(The figures indicate the number of semitones in each interval)

	Doubly Diminished	Diminished	Minor	Major	Augmented	Doubly Augmented
Second	C♯ – D𝄫 (1)	C♯ – D♭ (0)	C – D♭ (1)	C – D (2)	C – D♯ (3)	C – D𝄪 (4)
Third	C♯ – E𝄫 (1)	C♯ – E♭ (2)	C – E♭ (3)	C – E (4)	C – E♯ (5)	C – E𝄪 (6)
Sixth	C♯ – A𝄫 (6)	C♯ – A♭ (7)	C – A♭ (8)	C – A (9)	C – A♯ (10)	C – A𝄪 (11)
Seventh	C♯ – B𝄫 (8)	C♯ – B♭ (9)	C – B♭ (10)	C – B (11)	C – B♯ (12)	C – B𝄪 (13)

	Doubly Diminished	Diminished	Perfect	Augmented	Doubly Augmented
Prime	C – C𝄫 (2)	C – C♭ (1)	C – C (0)	C – C♯ (1)	C – C𝄪 (2)
Fourth	C♯ – F♭ (3)	C♯ – F (4)	C – F (5)	C – F♯ (6)	C – F𝄪 (7)
Fifth	C♯ – G♭ (5)	C♯ – G (6)	C – G (7)	C – G♯ (8)	C – G𝄪 (9)
Octave	C♯ – C♭ (10)	C♯ – C (11)	C – C (12)	C – C♯ (13)	C – C𝄪 (14)

TABLE IX

KEY SIGNATURES

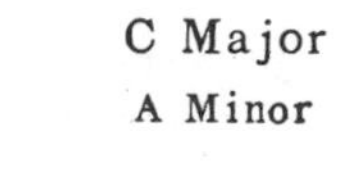

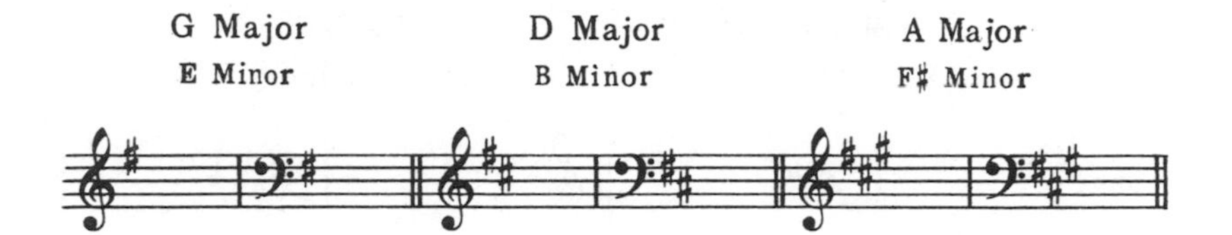

TABLE IX (continued)

KEY SIGNATURES

ORDER OF SHARPS AND FLATS

F C G D A E B

♯'s ⟶

⟵ ♭'s

TABLE X

SCALES AND MODES ★

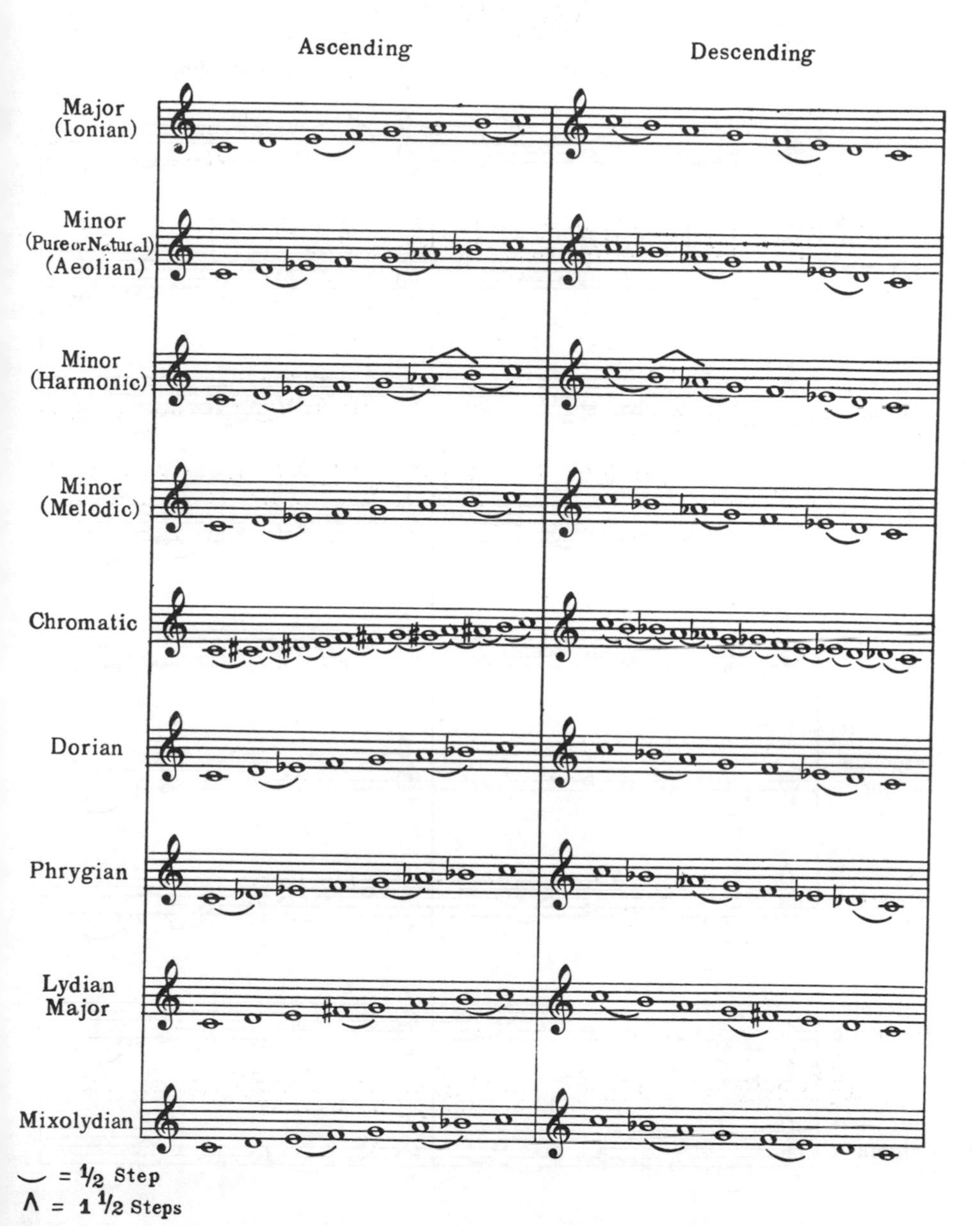

‿ = 1/2 Step
∧ = 1 1/2 Steps

★ In each example the starting note 'C' was chosen arbitrarily– The scales or modes may begin on any note encompassing one octave ascending and descending.

TABLE X (continued)

SCALES AND MODES

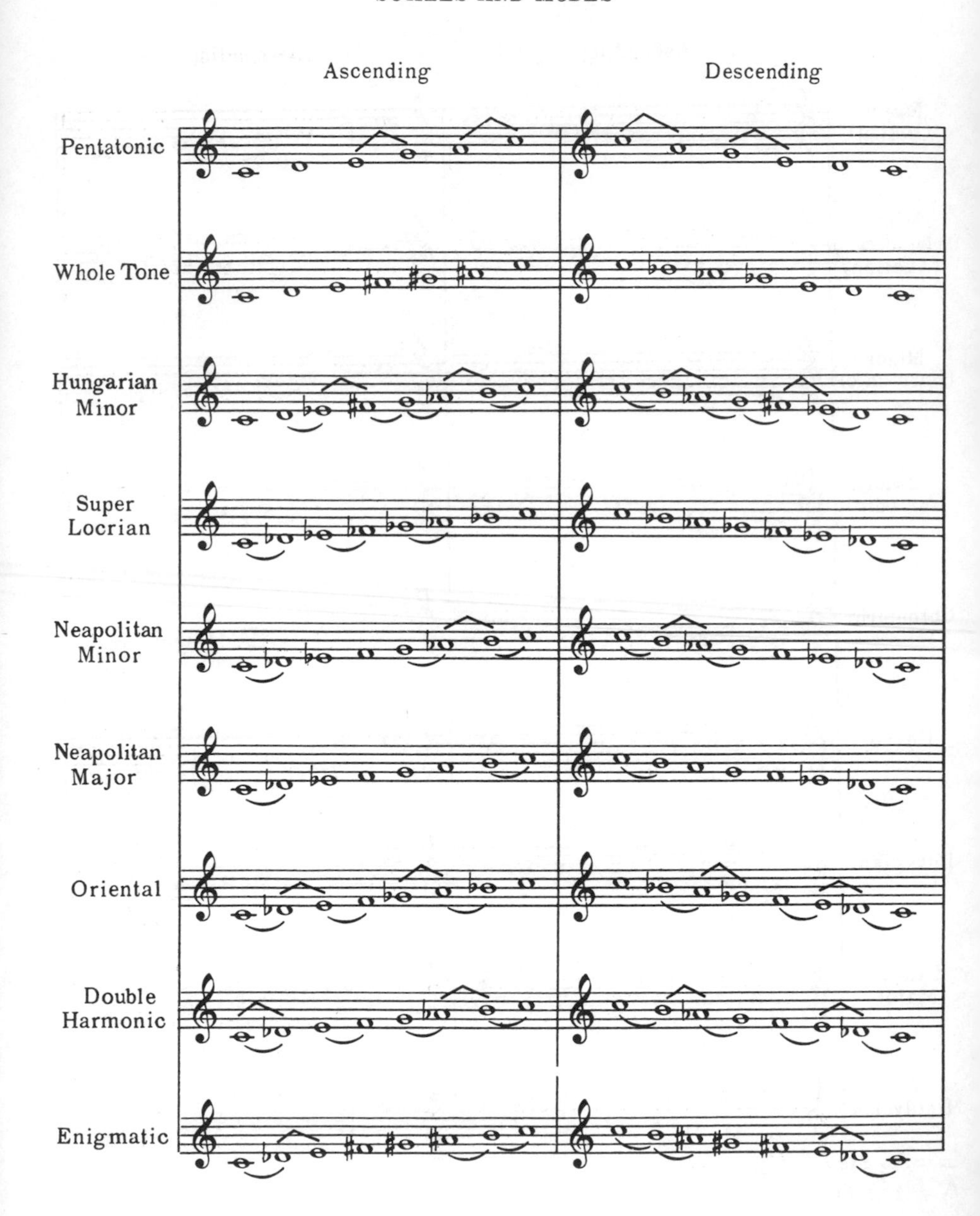

TABLE X (continued)

SCALES AND MODES

TABLE XI

NONHARMONIC TONES

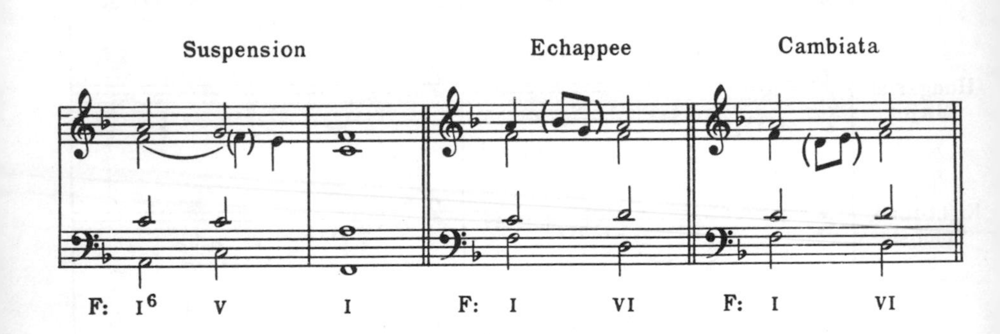

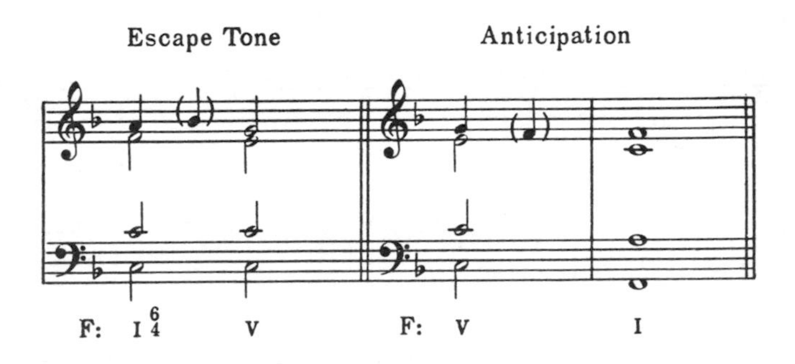

TABLE XII

MUSICAL ORNAMENTS

TABLE XII (continued)

MUSICAL ORNAMENTS

TABLE XIII

SIGNS

Pitch

Sign	Meaning	Sign	Meaning
(♩)	Note head	♮	Natural
(♩)	Note stem	𝄪	Double sharp
♪	Note flag	𝄫	Double flat
♪	Grace note	M	Major chord
8va	All' ottava	M(-)	Minor chord
8va basso	All' ottava	D(o)	Diminished chord
♯	Sharp	ø	Half-diminished 7th chord
♭	Flat	A(+)	Augmented chord

Dynamic

Sign	Meaning	Sign	Meaning
pp or *ppp*	Pianissimo	*ff* or *fff*	Fortissimo
p	Piano	*f*	Forte
mp	Mezzopiano	*mf*	Mezzoforte
>	Decrescendo (*Decr.*)	<	Crescendo (*Cresc.*)
>	Diminuendo (*Dim.*)	*sf*	Sforzato
< >	Messa Di Voce	*fp*	Forte-Piano

Rhythmic

Sign	Meaning	Sign	Meaning
¢	Alla Breve	𝄐	Fermata (Hold)
2/4	Meter Signature	//	Pause
Acc.	Accelerando	*Rit.*	Ritardando

TABLE XIII (continued)

SIGNS

Performance

Sign	Meaning	Sign	Meaning
> ∧	Accents	R *(m.d.)*	Right Hand
	Stressed and sustained	L *(m.g.)*	Left Hand
,	Breath mark	H	Heel or Horn
	Staccato	M	Hand, Manual or Metronome
	Intense staccato		Tie
	Portato		Repeated notes
⌒	Slur		Repeated notes
	Accented and sustained		Continuation of Trill Continuation of Octave mark
	Pesante, impressively		Arpeggio– broken chord
[	To be played with same finger or hand	Ped.	Loud pedal on piano
∧	Organ music, play with toes	*	Release the pedal
∪	Organ music, play with heel		Marking exactly the points of depressing and releasing the pedal
	Organ music, alternately heel and toe of same foot	⊓	Down Bow
	Change toes on organ pedal	V	Up Bow
	Slide same toe to next note	o	Harmonic
tr	Trill		Arpeggio or Arpeggiando
	Repeat sign		Tremolo or Roll

TABLE XIII (continued)

SIGNS

Performance

Tremolo legato

\|%\| Measure repeat sign

bis Repeat everything under bracket

Bracket (Brace)

A Stave

or Segno (Sign from which repeat is made)

ten. Tenuto

V. S. Volti subito Turn page quickly

Repeat

TABLE XIV

CHORD TYPES

Type	Abbreviation	Example
Major	M	
Minor	m	
Diminished	D	
Augmented	A	
Major-minor Seventh	Mm7	
Major-major Seventh (Major-Seventh)	M7	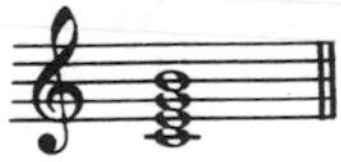
Minor-minor Seventh (Minor-Seventh)	m7	
Minor-major Seventh	mM7	
Diminished-minor Seventh	Dm7	
Diminished-diminished Seventh (Diminished-Seventh)	D7	
Augmented-major Seventh	AM7	
Augmented-minor Seventh	Am7	

TABLE XV

FORM

First Rondo Form

Principal Theme	Transition	Subordinate Theme	Re-transition	Principal Theme	Coda
Any Part-form		Different Key, usually related. (Codetta)		As before, possibly modified.	

Second Rondo Form

Principal Theme	Transition	I. Subordinate Theme	Re-transition	Codetta	Principal Theme	Transition	II. Subordinate Theme	Re-transition	Principal Theme	Coda
Any Part-form		Related key			As before, with possible, abbreviation		Remote key		As before or modified	

TABLE XV (continued)

Third Rondo Form

First Division			Middle Division	Recapitulation		
Prin. Th.	I. Sub. Th.	Prin. Th.	II. Sub. Th.	Prin. Th.	I. Sub. Th.	Prin. Th.
Any Part-form	Related key	Possibly abbreviated	Broader Form, remote key	As before	As before, Transposed	and Coda
Trans.	Re-trans.		Re-Trans.	Trans.		

Third Rondo Form with Development

First Division			Middle Division	Recapitulation		
Prin. Th.	I. Sub. Th.	Prin. Th.	Development	Prin. Th.	I. Sub. Th.	Prin. Th. and Coda

TABLE XV (continued)

Sonatina Form

Exposition			Recapitulation		
Prin. Theme Any part-form Transition	Sub. Theme Related key Codetta	Re-trans.	Prin. Theme As before Modified Transition	Sub. Theme Transposed to principal key Codetta	Coda

Enlarged Sonatina Form

Exposition			Recapitulation		
Prin. Theme	Sub. Theme Related key Codetta	Re-trans.	Prin. Theme Extended and developed	Sub. Theme Transposed Codetta	Coda

TABLE XV (continued)

Sonatina Form with final Da Capo

Exposition			Recapitulation		Extra Member	
Prin. Th.	Sub. Th. Related key	Re-trans.	Prin. Th.	Sub. Th. Transposed Re-transition	Prin. Th.	Coda

Sonata Allegro Form

Exposition			Development	Recapitulation			
Prin. Th. Any part-form Transition	Sub. Th. Related key	Codetta One or more	Sectional form Re-trans.	Prin. Th. As before Modified Trans.	Sub. Th. Transposed	Codetta	Coda

TABLE XV (continued)

Sonata Allegro Form with Development

: Exposition :		Development		Recapitulation		
Prin. Th.	Sub. Th.	Prin. Th. As before	- following sections	Prin. Th.	Sub. Theme	Coda

Abbreviated Sonata Allegro Form

Exposition		Development	Recapitulation	Coda
Prin. Th.	Sub. Th. Codetta	Re-transition	Subordinate Theme Transposed Codetta	

TABLE XV (continued)

Three-Part Song Form

Part I	Part II	Part III
Statement	Departure Return	Recurrence
Period-form Two phrases	Period or grouped-form	Period Codetta

The forms included herein are those which are most generally accepted and adaptable to structures of traditional nature. The reader is urged to pursue the study of form in volumes dedicated to this topic. Special investigation should be made into all binary and ternary forms, song forms, rondos, orchestral forms, dance and piano forms, vocal forms, contrapuntal forms and established forms of contemporary nature.

TABLE XVI

VOICE RANGES AND TYPES

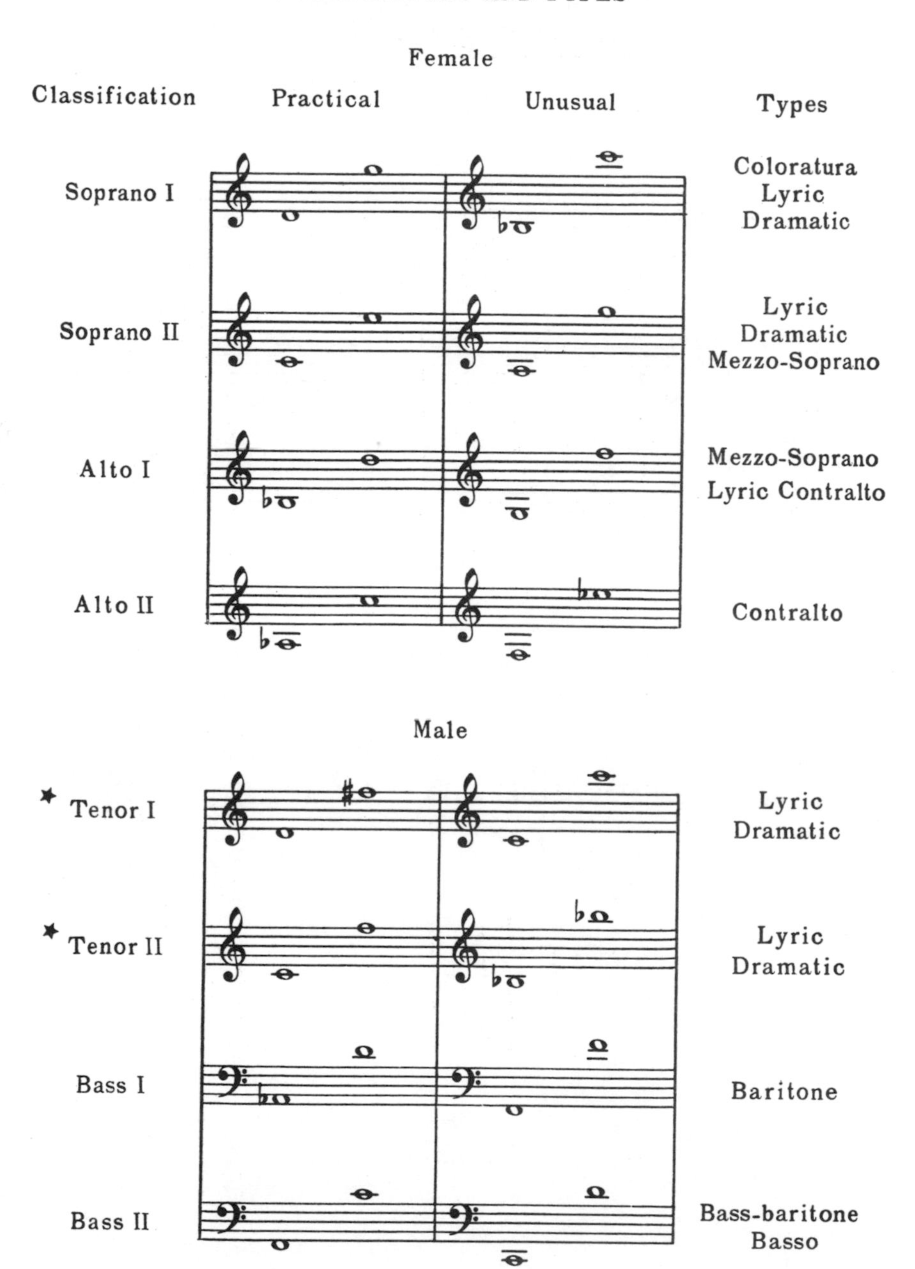

ounding one octave lower than written

TABLE XVII

STRING INSTRUMENT RANGES AND TRANSPOSITIONS

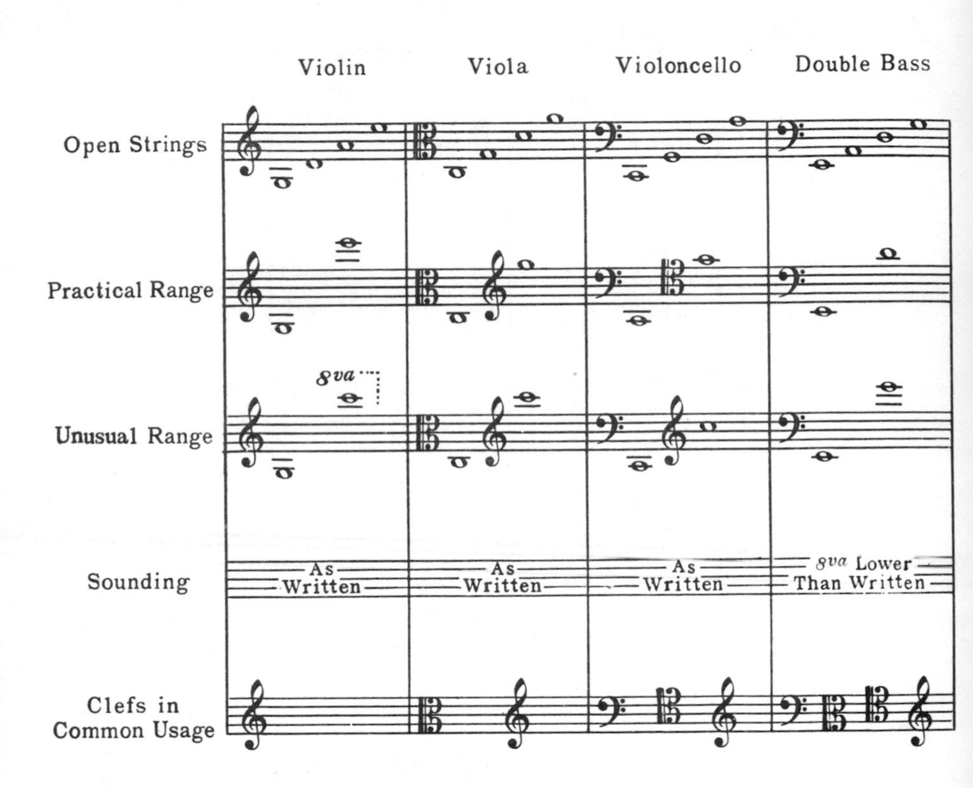

TABLE XVIII[A]

WIND INSTRUMENT RANGES AND TRANSPOSITIONS

The Woodwinds

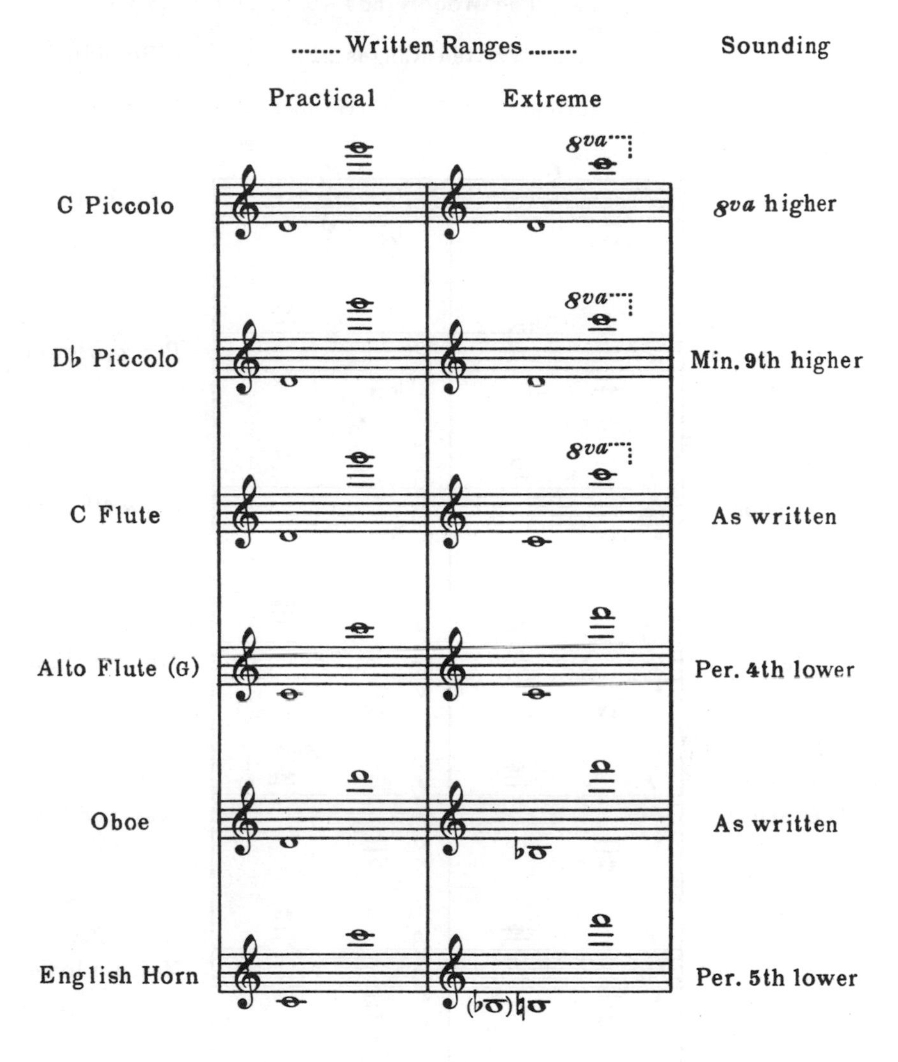

TABLE XVIII^A (continued)

The Woodwinds

	........Written Ranges........		Sounding
	Practical	Extreme	
Bassoon			As written
Contrabassoon			Per. *8va* lower
Sarrusophone			*8va* & 6th lower
E♭ Clarinet			Min. 3rd Higher
* B♭ Clarinet		*8va*	Maj. 2nd lower
E♭ Alto Clarinet			Maj. 6th lower
B♭ Bass Clarinet		**	Maj. 9th lower

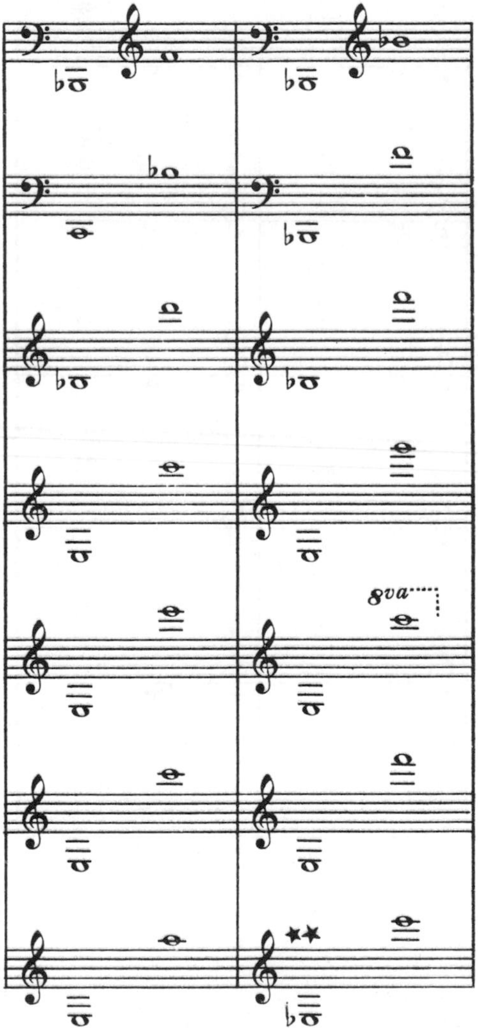

* Instruments pitched in other keys have similar ranges

** Not always available on every model or make

TABLE XVIII^A (continued)

The Woodwinds

	........Written Ranges........		Sounding
	Practical	Extreme	
E♭ Contrabass Clarinet		*	*8va* & Maj. 6th lower
B♭ Contrabass Clarinet		*	15ma & Maj. 2nd lower
B♭ Soprano Saxophone		SAME	Maj. 2nd lower
E♭ Alto Saxophone			Maj. 6th lower
B♭ Tenor Saxophone			Maj. 9th lower
E♭ Baritone Saxophone		SAME	*8va* & Maj. 6th lower
B♭ Bass Saxophone		SAME	15ma & Maj. 2nd lower

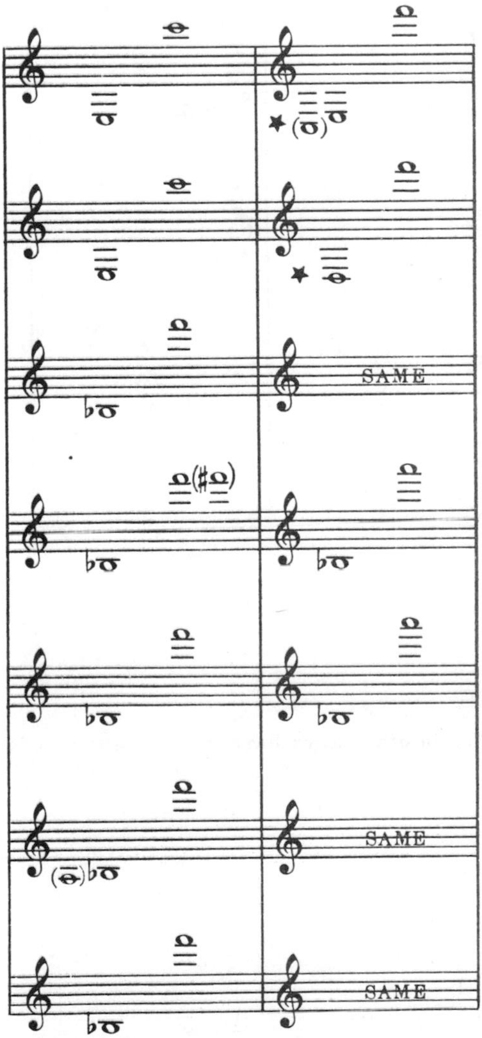

* Varies with make of instrument

TABLE XVIII[B]

The Brasses

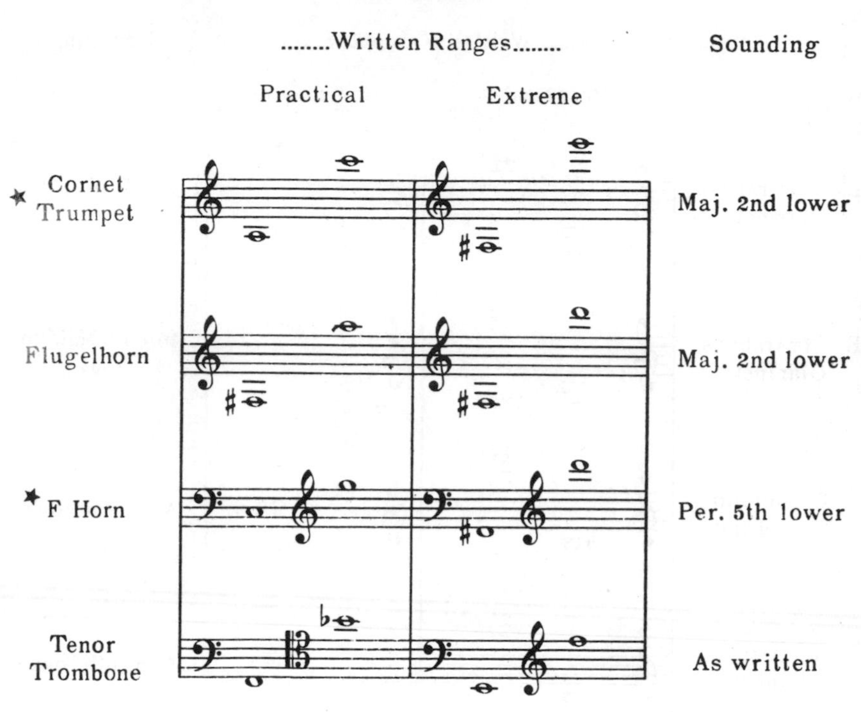

* Instruments pitched in other keys have similar ranges

TABLE XVIII[B] (continued)

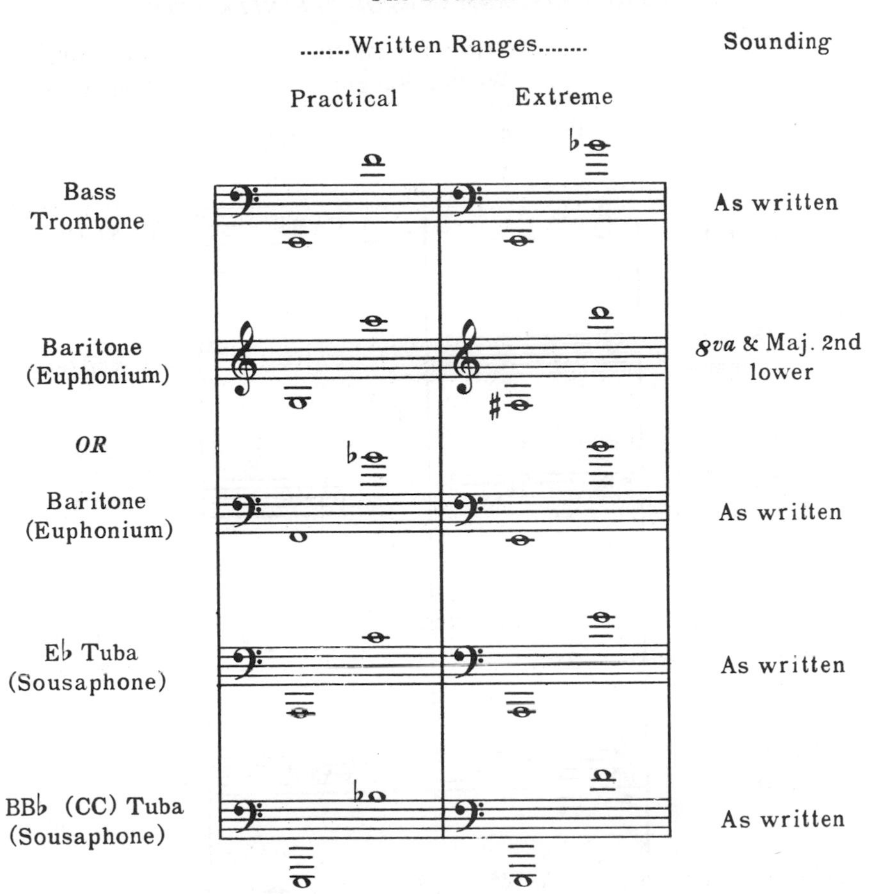

TABLE XVIII[c]

PERCUSSION INSTRUMENTS OF DEFINITE PITCH

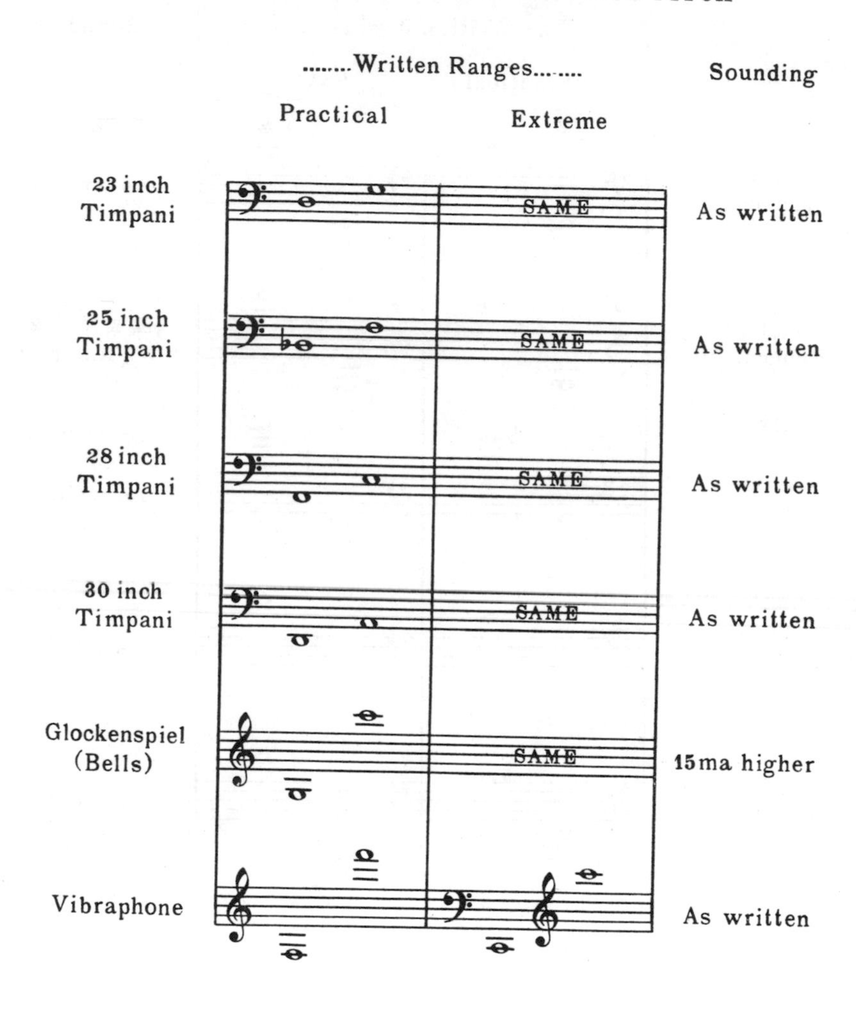

TABLE XVIII[c] (continued)

PERCUSSION INSTRUMENTS OF DEFINITE PITCH

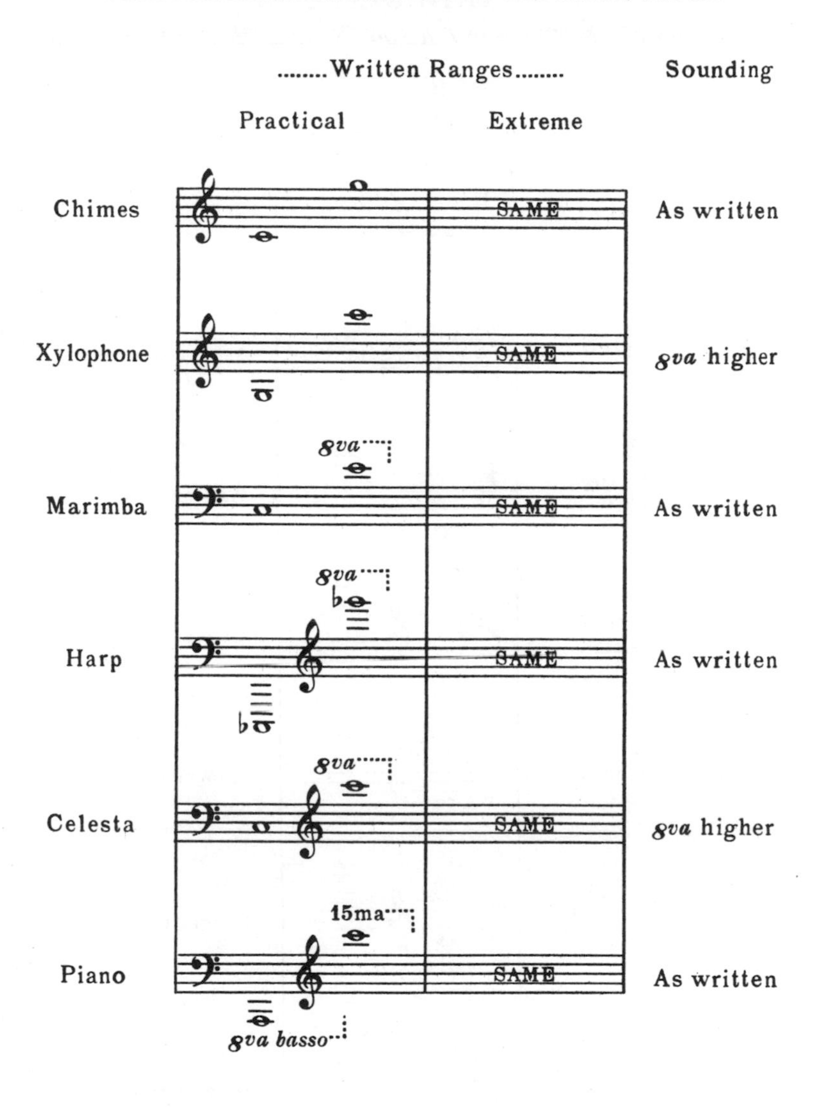

TABLE XIX

ADDITIONAL INSTRUMENT RANGES AND TRANSPOSITIONS

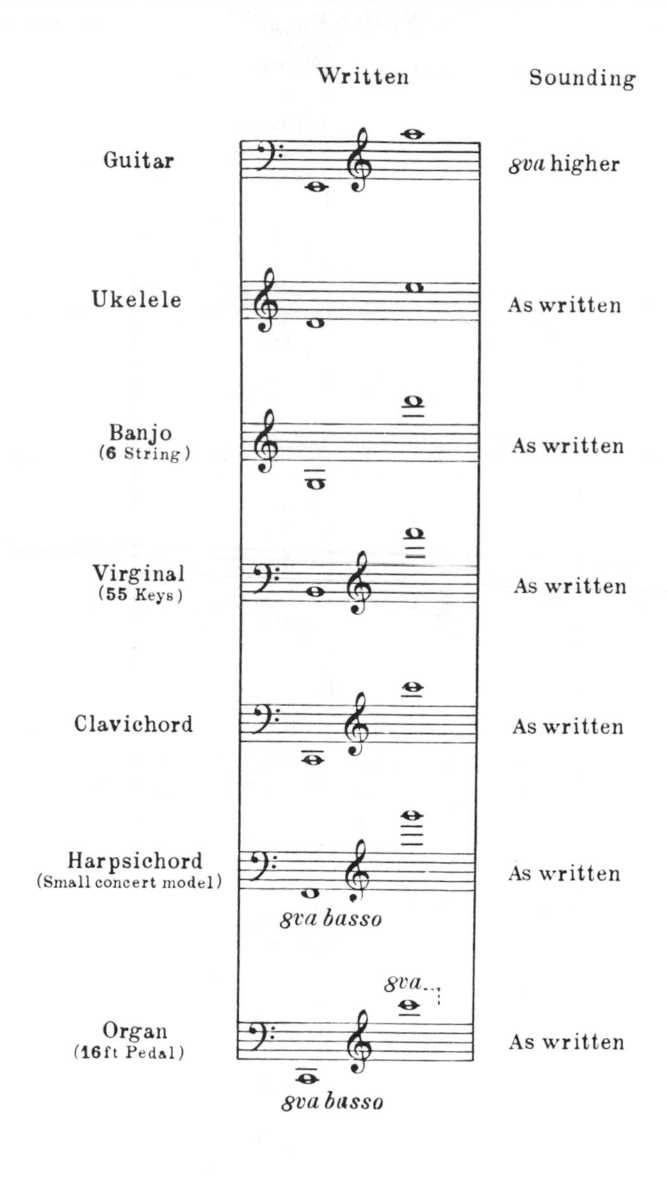

TABLE XX

VOICE AND INSTRUMENT RANGES COMPARED WITH PIANO KEYBOARD

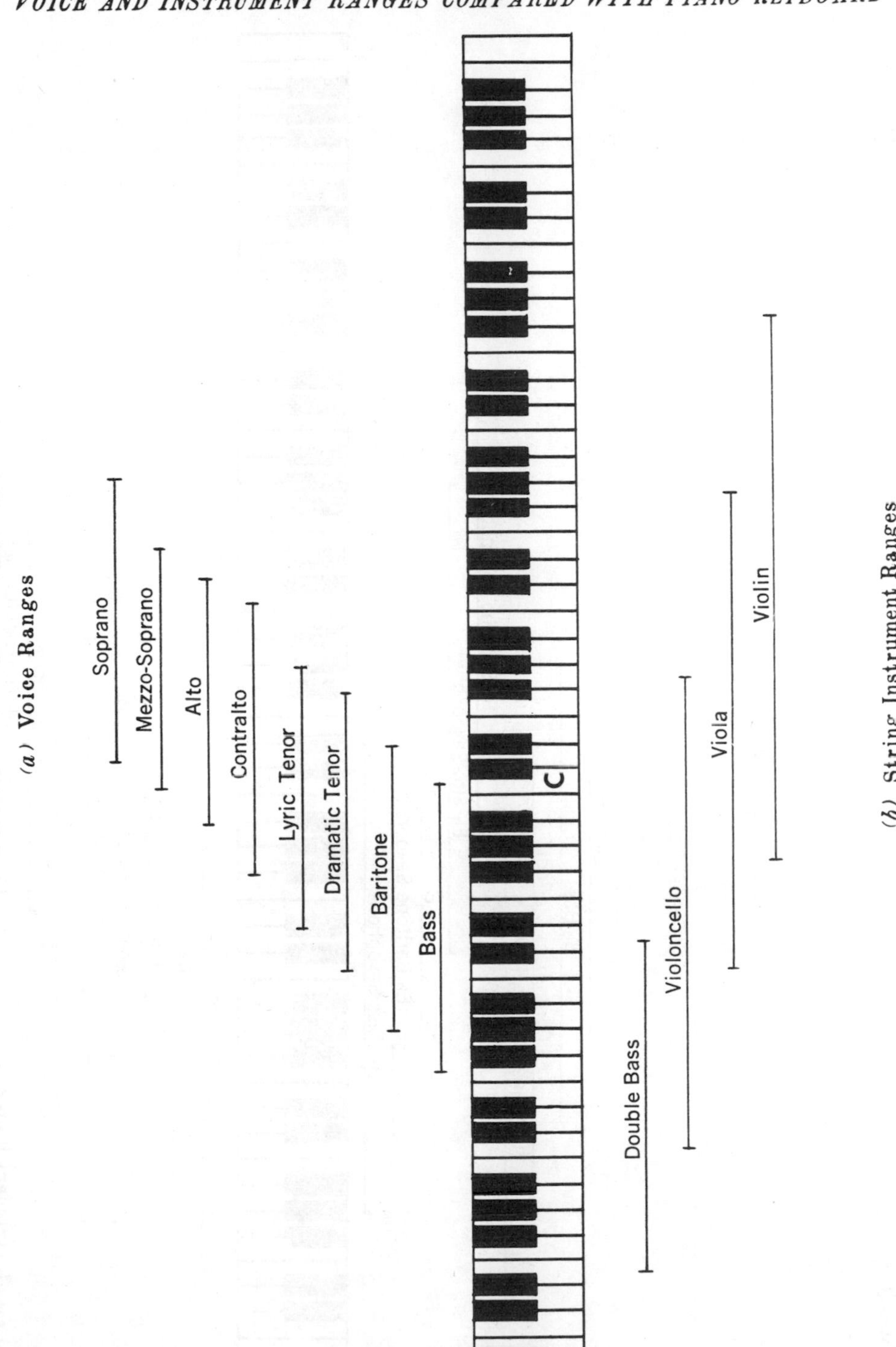

TABLE XX (continued)

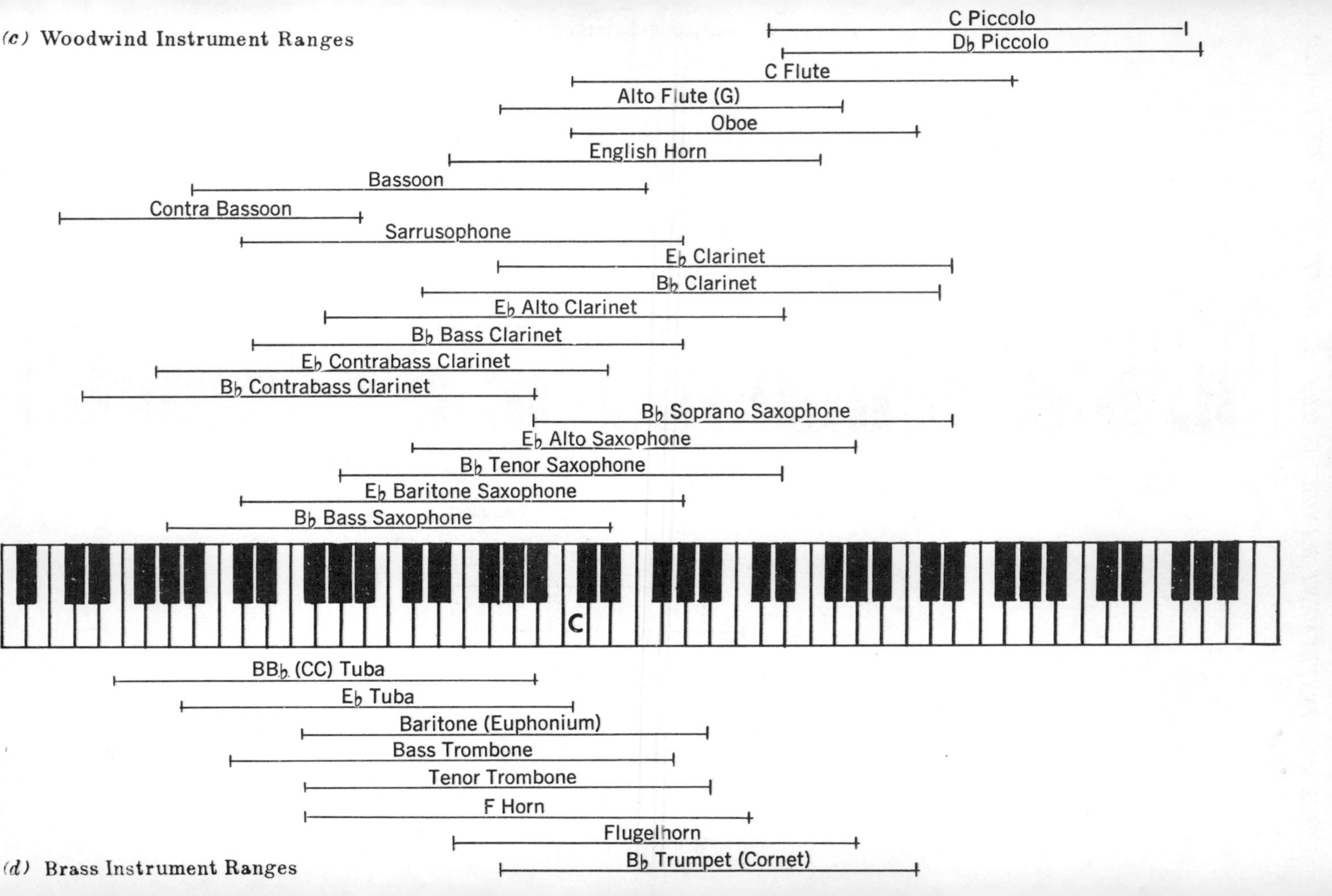

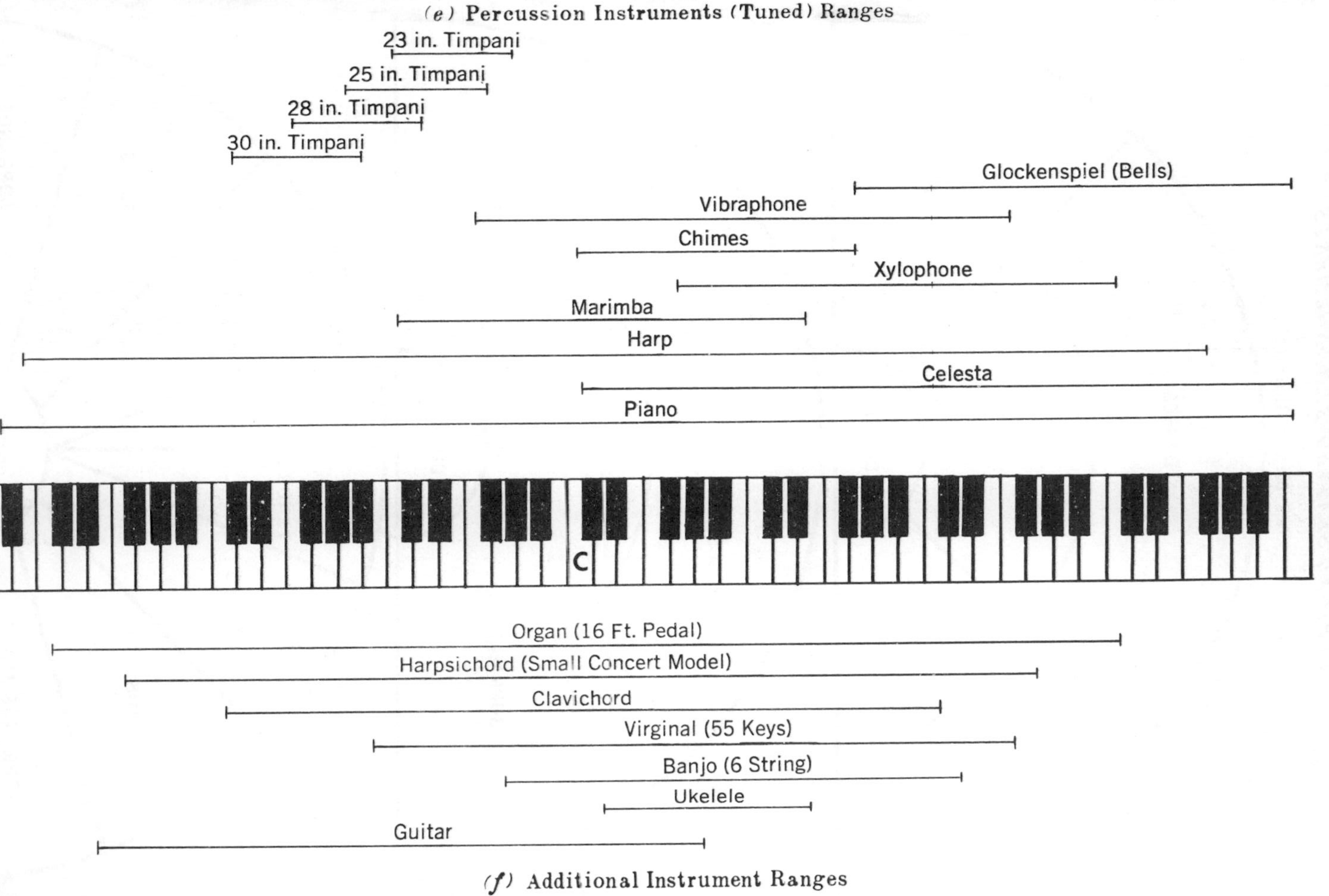
(e) Percussion Instruments (Tuned) Ranges
23 in. Timpani
25 in. Timpani
28 in. Timpani
30 in. Timpani
Glockenspiel (Bells)
Vibraphone
Chimes
Xylophone
Marimba
Harp
Celesta
Piano
C
Organ (16 Ft. Pedal)
Harpsichord (Small Concert Model)
Clavichord
Virginal (55 Keys)
Banjo (6 String)
Ukelele
Guitar
(f) Additional Instrument Ranges

TABLE XXI

TYPICAL SEATING ARRANGEMENTS

(a) Mixed Chorus

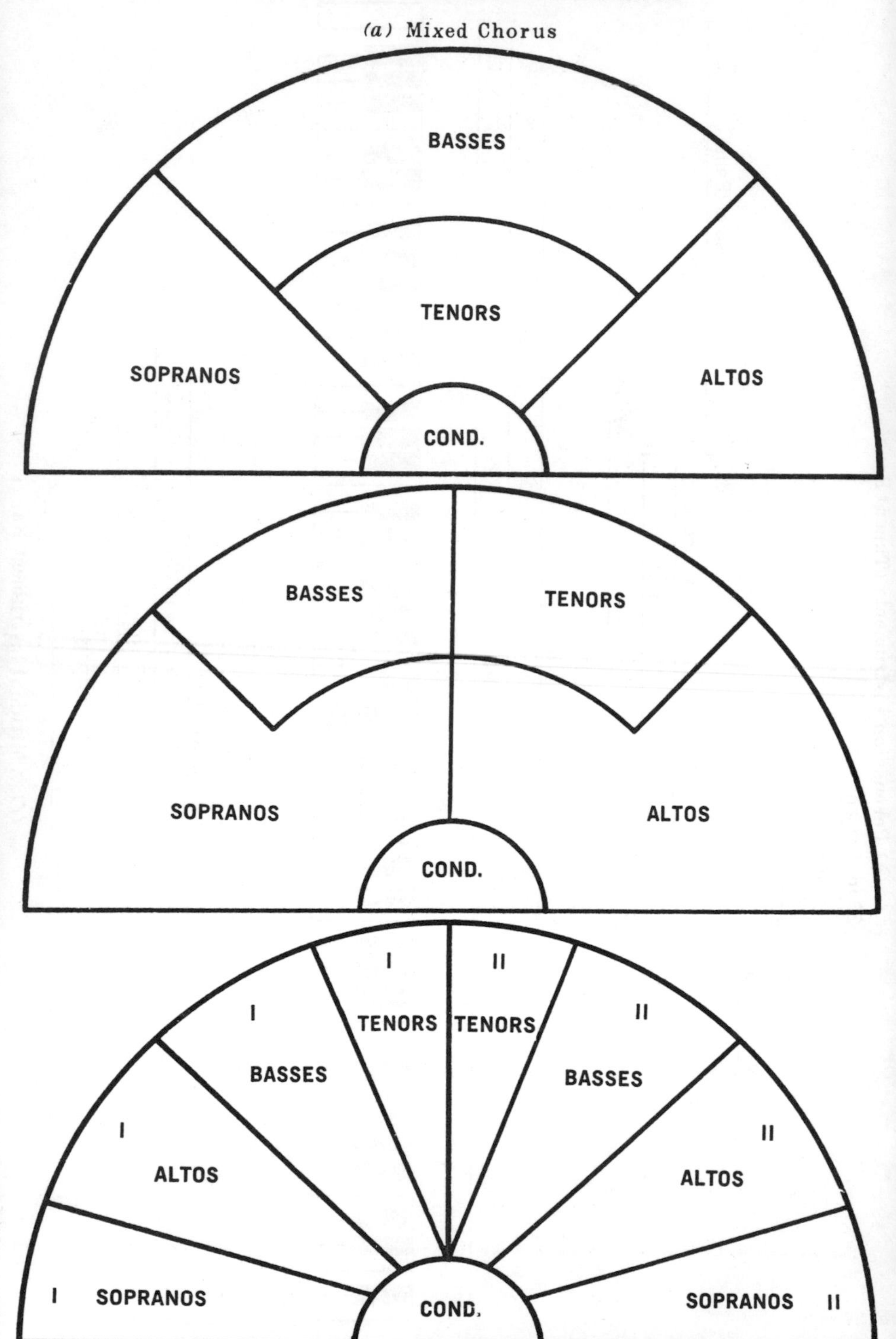

TABLE XXI (continued)

TYPICAL SEATING ARRANGEMENTS

(*b*) The Orchestra

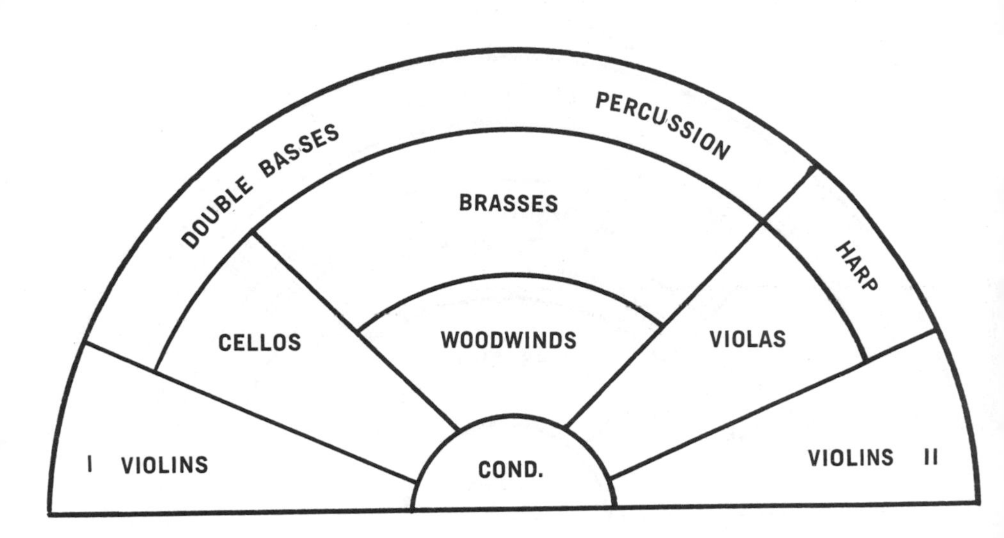

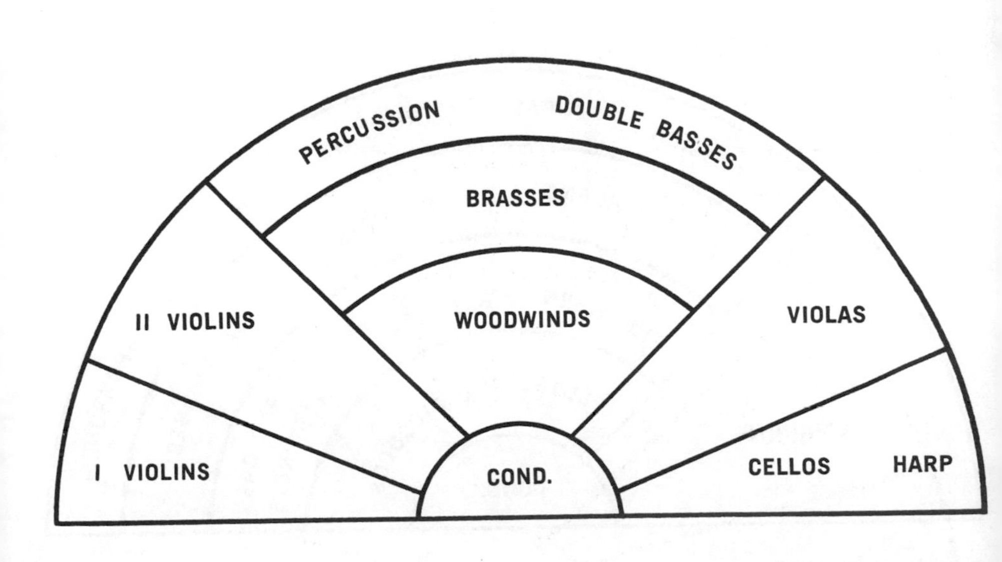

TABLE XXI (continued)

TYPICAL SEATING ARRANGEMENTS

(c) The Band

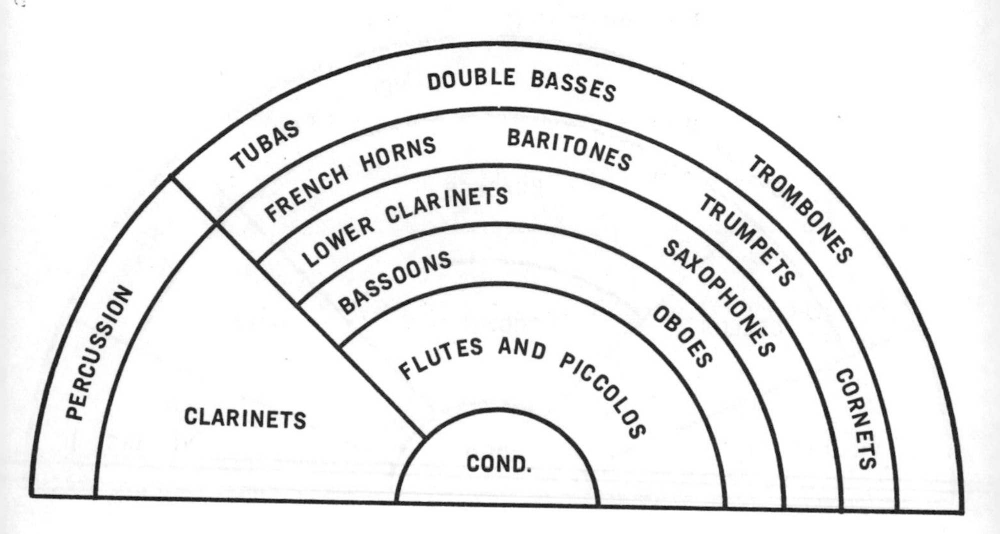

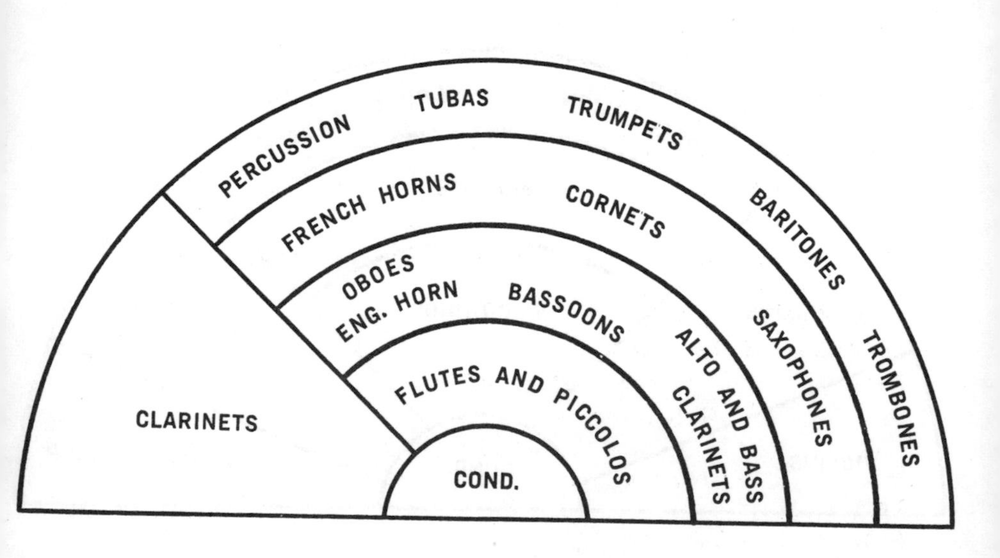

TABLE XXII

HIGHLIGHTS OF MUSIC IN HISTORY

The Polyphonic Period	**(800-1600)**
The Baroque Period	**(1600-1750)**
The Classical Period	**(1750-1820)**
The Romantic Period	**(1820-1900)**
The Scientific Period	**(1900-)**

1600 BEGINNING OF BAROQUE PERIOD
1602 Birth of Cavalli
1603 Death of Morley
1604 Francis Bacon: *Advancement of Learning*
1606 Birth of William Davenant
1610 Louis XIII - King of France
1612 Death of Gabrieli
1613 Death of Gesualdo
1616 Death of Shakespeare
1618 Beginning of 30 Year's War
1620 Francis Bacon: *Novum Organum*
1621 Dutch West India Co. founded
1623 Death of Weelkes and William Byrd
1625 Death of Gibbons
1628 Death of John Bull
1631 Rembrandt settled in Amsterdam
1633 Death of Peri — Birth of Lully
1635 Establishment of French Academy of Language and Literature
1638 Death of Wilbye
1642 English Civil Wars
1643 Death of Monteverdi
1644 Descartes: *Principles of Philosophy*
1647 Birth of Pelham Humfrey
1648 Treaty of Westphalia - End of 30 Year's War
1649 Execution of Charles I
1653 Birth of Corelli
1654 Death of Samuel Scheidt
1659 Birth of Purcell and A. Scarlatti

1661 Beginning rule of Louis XIV
1664 Black Death — Bubonic Plague sweeps London
1665 Bernini rebuilds the Louvre Palace
1666 Academy of Sciences established in Paris
1667 Milton's *Paradise Lost*
1668 Death of Davenant
1669 Paris Opera established by Lully
1672 Death of Schutz
1674 Death of Humfrey
1676 Death of Cavalli
1680 Birth of Vivaldi
1683 Birth of D. Scarlatti and Rameau
1685 Birth of J. S. Bach and Handel
1687 Death of Lully — Newton: *Law of Gravity*
1688 Versailles Palace completed
1689 Purcell: *Dido and Aeneas*
1690 Locke: *Essay Concerning Human Understanding*
1692 Salem witch trials
1695 Death of Purcell
1698 Lotti: *Mass VII*
1701 Founding of Yale University
1708 Death of John Blow
1709 Steele: *The Tatler*
1710 Wren: St. Paul's Cathedral (London)
1712 Bach: *Toccata and Fugue* (D minor)
1714 Birth of K. P. E. Bach and Gluck
1715 Death of Louis XIV
1717 Bach: *Passacaglia and Fugue* (C minor)
1719 Defoe: *Robinson Crusoe*
1721 Bach: *Brandenberg Concertos*
1722 Bach: *Well-Tempered Clavier*
1725 Death of A. Scarlatti
1726 Swift: *Gulliver's Travels*
1728 Gay: *The Beggar's Opera*
1729 Bach: *St. Matthew Passion*
1732 Birth of Haydn
1734 Pope: *Essay on Man*
1735 Birth of J. C. Bach
1738 Bach: *Mass in B Minor*
1740 Chardin: *The Blessing*
1742 Handel: *Messiah*
1743 Death of Vivaldi
1748 Bach: *Art of Fugue*
1749 Fielding: *Tom Jones*

1750 **BEGINNING OF CLASSICAL PERIOD** — Death of J. S. Bach
1756 Birth of Mozart
1757 Death of D. Scarlatti
1758 Defeat of British at Ticonderoga
1759 Death of Handel — Voltaire: *Candide*
1760 Birth of Cherubini
1762 Mozart: *Minuet and Trio for Piano*
1763 End of French and Indian War
1764 Death of Rameau
1765 Watt: Steam Engine — Hargreaves: Spinning Jenny
1766 Goldsmith: *The Vicar of Wakefield*
1770 Birth of Beethoven
1772 Fragonard: *Storming the Citadel*
1773 Boston Tea Party
1776 Declaration of Independence
1781 Surrender of Cornwallis at Yorktown
1782 Death of J. C. Bach — Birth of Auber
1785 Mozart: 6 String Quartets
1786 Birth of Weber — Mozart: *The Marriage of Figaro*
1787 Death of Gluck
1788 Death of K. P. E. Bach
1789 French Revolution
1790 Haydn: *String Quartet in D*
1791 Death of Mozart — Birth of Meyerbeer
1792 Birth of Rossini
1793 Whitney: Cotton gin
1794 Condorcet: *Progress of the Human Spirit*
1797 Birth of Donizetti and Schubert
1798 Coleridge: *Rime of the Ancient Mariner*
1799 Birth of Halevy
1800 Beethoven: *Symphony No. 1*
1801 Birth of Bellini
1803 Birth of Berlioz — Louisiana Purchase
1804 Birth of Glinka — Napoleon crowned Emperor
1805 Beethoven: *Fidelio*
1807 Fulton: Steamboat "Clermont"
1808 Goethe: *Faust*
1809 Death of Haydn — Birth of Mendelssohn
1810 Birth of Chopin and Schumann
1811 Birth of Liszt
1812 Beethoven: *Symphony No. 7*
1813 Birth of Verdi and Wagner
1814 Stephenson: Steam locomotive
1815 Defeat of Napoleon at Waterloo
1818 Birth of Gounod — Byron: *Childe Harold's Pilgrimage*

1820 BEGINNING OF ROMANTIC PERIOD
Keats: *Ode on a Grecian Urn* — Scott: *Ivanhoe*
1821 Death of Napoleon
1822 Birth of Franck — Schubert: *Unfinished Symphony*
1823 Monroe Doctrine
1824 Birth of Smetana and Bruckner
1825 Birth of Johann Strauss
1826 Death of Weber — Cooper: *The Last of the Mohicans*
1827 Death of Beethoven
1828 Death of Schubert
1830 Berlioz: *Symphonie Fantastique*
1833 Birth of Borodin and Brahms
1835 Death of Bellini — Birth of Saint-Saens
1838 Birth of Bizet
1839 Birth of Mussorgsky and Paine
1840 Birth of Tchaikovsky
1841 Birth of Dvorak — Emerson: *Essays*
1842 Birth of Massenet — Death of Cherubini
1843 Birth of Grieg
1844 Birth of Rimsky-Korsakov
1845 Birth of Faure — Poe: *The Raven*
1846 Mendelssohn: *Elijah*
1847 Death of Mendelssohn
1848 Death of Donizetti — Marx and Engel's *Communist Manifesto*
1849 Death of Chopin — California goldrush
1850 Hawthorne: *The Scarlet Letter*
1851 Melville: *Moby Dick*
1852 Stowe: *Uncle Tom's Cabin*
1853 Admiral Perry opens Japan
1854 Cornelius: *Ein Ton*
1855 Whitman: *Leaves of Grass*
1856 Death of Schumann
1857 Death of Glinka — Flaubert: *Madame Bovary*
1858 Birth of Leoncavallo and Puccini
1859 Birth of Herbert — Darwin: *The Origin of Species* — Wagner: *Tristan und Isolde*
1860 Birth of Mahler
1861 Birth of MacDowell — Beginning of U.S. Civil War
1862 Death of Halevy — Birth of Debussy
1863 Birth of Mascagni and Parker
1864 Death of Meyerbeer — Birth of Richard Strauss
1865 Birth of Sibelius — End of U.S. Civil War
1866 Whittier: *Snow Bound*
1867 Mussorgsky: *A Night on Bare Mountain*
1868 Death of Rossini

1869 Death of Berlioz — Blackmore: *Lorna Doone*
1870 Franco-Prussian War
1871 Death of Auber
1872 Tennyson: *Idylls of the King*
1873 Birth of Rachmaninoff
1874 Birth of Ives and Schoenberg
1875 Death of Bizet — Birth of Gliere and Ravel
1876 Birth of Falla — Bell: The telephone — First Bayreuth Festival
1877 Birth of Dohnanyi
1878 Hardy: *Return of the Native*
1879 Birth of Respighi — Edison: Electric light
1880 Birth of Arthur Shepherd
1881 Death of Mussorgsky — Birth of Bartok
1882 Birth of Stravinsky
1883 Death of Wagner — Birth of Webern
1884 Death of Smetana — Birth of Griffes
1885 Birth of Berg
1886 Death of Liszt — Merganthaler: Linotype
1887 Death of Borodin
1888 Rimsky-Korsakov: *Scheherazade*
1889 Van Gogh: *Starry Night*
1890 Death of Franck — Renoir: *In the Meadow*
1891 Birth of Prokofiev
1892 Birth of Milhaud and Honegger
1893 Death of Gounod and Tchaikovsky
1894 Birth of Piston
1895 Birth of Hindemith — Roentgen: X-ray
1896 Death of Bruckner — Birth of Hanson, Sessions and Thomson
1897 Death of Brahms
1898 Birth of Cowell, Gershwin and Harris — Spanish-American War
1899 Death of Johann Strauss — Birth of Poulenc — Sibelius: *Finlandia*

1900 BEGINNING OF SCIENTIFIC PERIOD
Birth of Copland, Krenek, Weill, Antheil, Luening — Boxer Rebellion in China
1901 Death of Verdi — Birth of Poot, Partch — Rachmaninoff: *Piano Concerto No. 2* — President McKinley assassinated
1902 Debussy: *Pelleas et Melisande* — Founding of Ford Motor Company
1903 Birth of Khatchaturian, Giannini — Wright brothers: First airplane flight
1904 Birth of Kabalevsky — Puccini: *Madame Butterfly* — Russo-Japanese War
1905 Birth of Blitzstein, Lambert — Death of Dvorak — Freud: *Psychoanalysis*
1906 Birth of Creston, Finney, Shostakovich, Lockwood — Death of Paine — San Francisco earthquake
1907 Birth of Badings, Phillips — Death of Grieg — H. Rousseau: *The Snake Charmer* — William James: *Pragmatism*

1908 Birth of Carter, Ayala — Death of Rimsky-Korsakov, MacDowell — Model T Ford produced

1909 Marconi: Development of wireless radio — Peary reaches North Pole

1910 Birth of Barber, Jones — Picasso: *Girl with a Mandolin*

1911 Birth of Menotti, Hovhaness — Death of Mahler — R. Strauss: *Der Rosenkavalier* — Mexican Revolution

1912 Birth of Markevitch, Cage, Barlow, Moncayo—Death of Massenet—Ravel: *Daphnis et Chloe* — Titanic sunk

1913 Birth of Britten, Dello Joio, Gould — Stravinsky: *Le Sacre du Printemps* — Federal Income Tax in U.S.

1914 Birth of Kubik, Mills—Outbreak of World War I—Completion of Panama Canal

1915 Birth of Schuman, Diamond, Fine, Persichetti—Lusitania sunk—Einstein: *Theory of Relativity*

1916 Birth of Weber, Babbitt, Ginastera — Sandburg: *Chicago Poems*

1917 Birth of Kay, Ward, Harrison — Prohibition Amendment — Russian Revolution

1918 Birth of Bernstein — Death of Debussy — End of World War I

1919 Birth of Kirchner — Death of Leoncavallo, Parker — Treaty of Versailles

1920 Birth of Maderna, Shapero — Death of Griffes — League of Nations — First radio broadcasting station

1921 Birth of Kurka, Imbrie — Death of Saint-Saens — Peace Treaty signed with Germany

1922 Birth of Foss — Joyce: *Ulysses* — Mussolini marches on Rome

1923 Birth of Mennin, Powell, Rorem, Kraft — Stravinsky: *Les Noces* — Hitler: *Mein Kampf*

1924 Death of Faure, Puccini, Herbert, and Lenin at age 54

1925 Birth of Boulez, Schuller — Berg: *Wozzeck* — Scopes Trial

1926 Birth of Henze, Floyd, Schifrin — Hemingway: *The Sun Also Rises*

1927 Ravel: *Bolero* — Lindbergh's solo flight — Teapot Dome Scandal

1928 First radio broadcast of New York Philharmonic—Gershwin: *An American in Paris* — Birth of Karlheinz Stockhausen

1929 Stock market collapse: The Great Depression

1930 Shostakovich: *The Golden Age* — Penicillin discovered

1931 Ravel: *Piano Concerto for the Left Hand* — Japan invades Manchuria — Empire State Building completed

1932 Birth of Levy — Gershwin: *Cuban Overture* — F.D.R. elected

1933 Birth of Blackwood, Layton — Prohibition repealed — Hitler: Chancellor of Germany

1934 Prokofiev: *Lieutenant Kije* — Hitler becomes Fuehrer

1935 Death of Berg and Will Rogers

1936 Death of Respighi—Mitchell: *Gone With The Wind*—Sulfa drugs introduced in U.S.

1937 Death of Ravel, Gershwin — Amelia Earhart lost in Pacific

1938 Hindemith: *Mathis der Maler*—Chamberlain promises "peace in our time."

1939 Hitler's invasion of Poland: World War II begins

1940 Germans enter Paris — Trotsky assassinated in Mexico
1941 Japanese attack on Pearl Harbor: U.S. enters the war
1942 Britten: *A Ceremony of Carols* — First nuclear chain reaction by Fermi
1943 Death of Rachmaninoff — Bartok: *Concerto for Orchestra* — Roosevelt approves Withholding Income Tax — Race Riots in Detroit
1944 Bernstein: *Fancy Free* — MacArthur returns to Philippines
1945 Death of Mascagni, Bartok, Webern—End of World War II—First Atomic Bomb
1946 Death of Falla — Sessions: *Symphony No. 2* — Nuremburg Trials
1947 Truman Doctrine — Taft-Hartley Act
1948 W. Schuman: *Symphony No. 6* — Ghandi assassinated — Alger Hiss case
1949 Death of Richard Strauss — U.S.S.R. explodes atomic bomb
1950 Beginning of Korean War — U.S. plans hydrogen bomb
1951 Death of Schoenberg — Menotti: *Amahl and the Night Visitors* — Truce talks in Korea
1952 Hemingway: *The Old Man and the Sea* — George VI dies — Stockhausen: *Electronic Studies* — Eisenhower elected President
1953 Death of Prokofiev and Stalin — Armistice in Korea
1954 Death of Ives — Hanson: *Sinfonia Sacra* — First Atomic Sub: *Nautilus*
1955 Death of Honegger, Enesco — Churchill, at 80, succeeded by Eden — Salk serum perfected
1956 Death of Gliere — Uprising in Hungary — First man-made satellite
1957 Death of Sibelius—Stravinsky: *Agon*—Stockhausen: *Gruppen*—Sputnik I
1958 Death of Ralph V. Williams — Barber: *Vanessa* — Boulez: *Poesie pour Pouvoir* — Nobel Prize to Pasternak for *Doctor Zhivago*
1959 Death of Villa-Lobos — Castro victorious over Batista — Khrushchev visits U.S. — Quiz Show investigations
1960 Death of Dohnanyi — U-2 plane shot down in Russia — Kennedy elected President
1961 First manned space flights
1962 Death of Ibert
1963 Death of Poulenc, Hindemith — President Kennedy assassinated
1964 Congress passes bill to establish National Cultural Center
1965 Private and public funds made available in support of composers—Gemini IV and V launched.